RADICAL

IN THE

RADICAL LONDON
IN THE 1950S

David Mathieson

AMBERLEY

Front cover: From footage supplied by British Pathé.

First published 2016

Amberley Publishing
The Hill, Stroud
Gloucestershire, GL5 4EP

www.amberley-books.com

Copyright © David Mathieson, 2016

The right of David Mathieson to be identified as the Author of this work has been asserted in accordance with the Copyrights, Designs and Patents Act 1988.

ISBN 978 1 4456 6103 2 (print)
ISBN 978 1 4456 6104 9 (ebook)

British Library Cataloguing in Publication Data. A catalogue record for this book is available from the British Library.

Origination by Amberley Publishing
Printed in the UK.

CONTENTS

FOREWORD

In 1957, the prime minister, Harold Macmillan, coined a phrase that he hoped would sum up the period of his government – 'our people have never had it so good'. The problem was that for kids like me, growing up in Notting Hill, life was still far more of a struggle than Macmillan wanted to admit. True, the trauma of the Second World War was behind us and the Attlee government had made radical reforms. True, the country generally was becoming better off and a consumer boom was on the way. But, as those of us who lived in the capital at the time well knew, that was far from the whole picture. Families such as mine were increasingly left behind, trapped in a cycle of material poverty which Macmillan's phrase did not begin to describe or explain.

It was not much different in other parts of London like Holborn and St Pancras, the area covered by this book and a bus ride away from where I lived. That things were not so good for all was visible from much of the shoddy housing which lined countless streets in central London. Dilapidated, overcrowded buildings were common and slum landlords became notorious for exploiting tenants. Then, as now, finding a decent place to live at an affordable rent was the big concern for many Londoners. Rebuilding the city after the war was a complicated, painful process. Making good the damage from the Blitz, clearing Victorian slums and housing young families of the 'baby boom' generation was never going to be easy. Not surprisingly, there were many different views about the changes which were needed. In Holborn and St Pancras, the clash of ideas over housing and what London should look like led to an extraordinary breakdown of normal politics and some of the worst rioting ever seen in London. The 1950s are often held up as a golden age of political consensus but this well-researched book reveals a much more complex reality in London, which has too often been overlooked.

It is a timely moment to revisit this history because once again housing is at the top of the political agenda. Soaring rents and house prices in London mean that that there is a growing list of people – from surgeons to school teachers – who can no longer afford to live anywhere close to the communities which they serve. Stable neighbourhoods are breaking up. Sons and daughters cannot afford to live near and care for elderly parents. Corner shops shut down because they cannot afford to pay escalating rents and more public space, where gossip is swapped and friendships are forged, is lost. The current Tory proposals will do very little to help Generation Rent now and, as this book clearly illustrates, housing policies based on untrammelled market forces have never worked in London

Unfortunately, the book is opportune in another way too because it explains how splits, divisions and dogma on the left weakened the Labour Party as a credible electoral force during the 1950s. The Conservatives won three elections in a row and dominated the politics of the decade while a divided Labour Party was impotent, unable to properly protect the very people that it came into being to represent. The parallels with what is happening within Labour now are painfully obvious. For that reason alone this is a book well worth reading by anyone who wants to put the politics of today in their rightful historical context and learn from the mistakes of the past.

Rt Hon Alan Johnson MP

September 2016

TIMELINE

1945

May

The Labour Party wins the general election with a majority of 146. Clement Attlee replaces Churchill as prime minister.

October

The United Nations comes into existence.

1946

March

Churchill delivers a speech in Zurich in which he warns of an 'iron curtain' falling to dividing Europe. Second World War allies become enemies and enemies become allies.

May

The National Insurance Act lays the foundations for a 'cradle to grave' welfare state with comprehensive unemployment, sickness, maternity and widows' benefits.

1947

January

Nationalisation of the coal, gas and electricity industries.

August

India gains independence from Britain.

December

An exceptionally harsh winter is accompanied by a fuel shortage and financial crisis. A policy of austerity to cut public spending is introduced.

1948

June

Post-war immigration from the Commonwealth begins as the SS *Empire Windrush* arrives at Tilbury carrying nearly 500 Caribbean immigrants.

July

The National Health Service is established and becomes one of the most popular institutions in Britain, second only to the monarchy.

July

Berlin Airlift begins after Soviet forces blockade the city. In May 1949, the Soviets backed down and lifted their blockade.

July

Olympic Games open at Wembley Stadium in London – the so-called 'Austerity Games'.

1949

April

North Atlantic Treaty Organisation (NATO) founded.

June

George Orwell's novel *Nineteen Eighty-Four* is published.

1950

February

The Labour Party wins the general election with Clement Attlee returned as prime minister. His majority, however, is reduced from 146 to just five and the socialist vision of a post-war New Jerusalem fades.

August

British troops arrive to support US forces in the Korean War. Some 4 million people would die in the conflict.

1951
May
Festival of Britain is opened to try and sustain a mood of post-war optimism.
October
Conservatives win the general election with a majority of 17 and Winston Churchill becomes prime minister at the age of seventy-six.

1952
February
George VI dies.
June
Elizabeth II is crowned.

1953
April
The structure of DNA is discovered by Watson and Crick.
May
Blackpool win the FA Cup largely due to a brilliant performance from Stanley Mathews.
June
England regain the Ashes after winning the series against Australia for the first time since 1934.
March
Joseph Stalin dies.

1954
March
The USA tests a hydrogen bomb in the Pacific 1,000 times more powerful than the atom bombs dropped on Japan.
May
Roger Bannister runs a mile in under four minutes.

1955
April
Winston Churchill retires as prime minister and is succeeded by Sir Anthony Eden.
May
Eden calls a snap election which the Tories win by 345 seats to Labour's 277.
May
The USSR and satellite countries sign the Warsaw Pact agreement.
May
Rock 'n' roll is born with the release of Bill Hailey's 'Rock Around the Clock'.
September
Commercial television starts with the first ITV broadcast and the BBC monopoly is broken.
December
Hugh Gaitskell beats Nye Bevan to become leader of the Labour Party.

1956
February
'Cambridge spies' Burgess and Maclean surface in Moscow after disappearing in 1951.
May
John Osborne's play *Look Back in Anger* is staged and the 'Angry Young Men' are born.
October
Elvis Presley is launched as a mega-star with the film *Love Me Tender*.
July
Chronic pollution prompts the passing of the Clean Air Act. The Act was a response to the severe London smog of 1952, which killed more than 4,000 people.
July
Jim Laker takes nineteen Austrian wickets for ninety runs – an all-time record – in the test at Old Trafford.

October

The UK's first nuclear power station goes on line.

November

The Suez Crisis begins when Britain and France invade Egypt after nationalisation of the Suez Canal.

1957

October

Russian satellite Sputnik 1 orbits the earth and the space race begins.

January

Sir Anthony Eden resigns as prime minister and is replaced by Harold Macmillan.

March

Ghana becomes the first British colony in Africa to gain independence and marked the rapid decolonisation in Africa.

May

Britain tests its first hydrogen bomb.

July

Rent Act passed to decontrol rents.

1958

February

The Campaign for Nuclear Disarmament is launched.

May

Shelagh Delaney's ground breaking play *A Taste of Honey*, dealing with interracial relationships, unmarried motherhood and homosexuality, has its first night.

May

St Pancras council flies the Red Flag from the town hall.

July

The first life peers enter the House of Lords.

August

The Notting Hill race riots break out.

December
The UK's first motorway system opens with the M6 Preston bypass and, soon after, the M1.

1959
August
The first Mini car goes on sale.
October
Conservatives under Harold Macmillan win the general election with 365 seats (49.3 per cent of the vote) to 258 for Labour.
November
Britain becomes a founder member of the European Free Trade Association (EFTA).
Labour-controlled London County Council open the Alton Estate in Roehampton, a model of post-war public housing.

1960
January
On a visit to Africa, Harold Macmillan describes a 'wind of change' blowing across the continent.
August
Cyprus gains independence from the UK.
August
The Beatles perform their first live concert under this name.
September
The first traffic wardens appear on the streets of London.
Riots in St Pancras over housing and rents.
December
The first episode of *Coronation Street* is screened by Granada TV.

1962
March
The Liberals win a sensational victory at the Orpington by-election and Harold Macmillan's popularity slumps.

July
Harold Macmillan engages in a radical Cabinet reshuffle – 'the night of the long knives'.

November
The first episode of the satirical *That Was the Week That Was* is screened.

1963

January
Labour leader Hugh Gaitskell dies suddenly aged fifty-six and is succeeded by Harold Wilson.

June
John Profumo, Secretary of State for War, resigns over his affair with Christine Keeler.

October
Harold Macmillan resigns on grounds of ill health and Sir Alec Douglas-Home becomes prime minister.

November
President Kennedy is assassinated.

1964

October
Labour wins the general election with 317 seats to 304 for the Conservatives. Harold Wilson becomes prime minister.

INTRODUCTION

At the end of 1960, Pathé News produced a review of the year's sporting, social and political highlights which was shown in cinemas across Britain. Along with the election of President John F. Kennedy, Prime Minister Harold Macmillan's 'winds of change' tour across Africa and the 'unforgettable loveliness' of Princess Margaret on her wedding day, the compilation included what the commentator described as 'anarchy' in St Pancras. A frame from Pathé's sequence is the cover photograph of this book – the man being arrested was one of thousands who took to the streets to protest about the evictions of two tenants in St Pancras.

Despite its importance at the time, this explosion of violence and the housing crisis that caused it has been passed over in many the more conventional accounts of post-war Britain. When it comes to writing up the past, it seems that these events have been thrown into the historical equivalent of an unmarked grave. Worse still, the government is determined that some elements of the story will remain buried in the face of efforts to disinter them. In 2016, I made several Freedom of Information requests (FOI) to find out more about the circumstances and characters behind the riots. Each FOI was firmly and politely declined by the Whitehall machine on grounds of national security. It is known that at least 250,000 communists and fellow travelling sympathisers were kept under MI5 surveillance in the 1950s. As will become clear from the evidence pieced together in this book, it is inconceivable that several of key players in St Pancras were not among them or that the security services did not keep a very close watch on what was happening in the area. Failure to have done so would have been inexplicably careless. The more pressing concern now is that the government refuses to publish any files – or even admit that they hold files – sixty years later.

Notwithstanding the lack of access to information collected and held in the public name, the story of central London in the post-war years remains compelling. Much has been told about the heroic resistance of London and its people during the Second World War but far less has been written about what happened next. The London described in this book is the fascinating story of the capital as it emerged from the rubble of the Blitz, with all the stresses and strains of reconstruction, to become the city we know today.

But this book is not just about history; it has a startling relevance for what is happening today. Then, as now, a dysfunctional London housing market was failing to achieve its basic objective: to provide decent homes for ordinary Londoners at a price they can afford. A frenzy of property speculation led to spiralling rents, a loss of security for tenants and increasingly desperate local authorities trying to help those most in need.

Then, as now, the Labour Party was failing too. Riven by splits and internal wrangling, it was divided about its vision for society and unclear about how it was going to lead there. Ordinary working people looked to Labour for protection in times of profound change but the party was not up to the task. The result was more than a decade of uninterrupted Conservative government over which Labour had neither control nor influence. The warning for Labour today could not be clearer.

This book is based material that I researched in the late 1980s for my PhD. During that time and later I worked as an adviser for two Labour MPs, Frank Dobson and the late Robin Cook. I was never sure how much they ever listened to my advice but

I certainly learned a lot from them and am truly grateful. Many people provided invaluable help and guidance during the writing and rewriting and I am especially thankful to my editor Alan Murphy, Professor Brendan Evans, Malcolm Holmes and the staff of the Camden Local History library, the London History Workshop, the British Library, Janet Dobson, Sally Gimson, Dinah Roake, Denis McShane, Victoria Hughes, Emma Leakey, Harry Schindler and Tim Whitworth. Between them they weeded out a mountain of errors in the drafts and those that remain are my fault alone. And once again my own insurgent rebels, Olivia and Ermias, demonstrated more patience than I had a right to expect from them. Thank you.

Holborn, September 2016

Chapter 1

A NATIONAL DISGRACE AND
A NATIONAL DISASTER

The Rebuilding of London after the Blitz and the London Property Boom

At dawn on 21 September 1960, bailiffs crashed through the roofs of two council flats in the St Pancras district of central London. After hours of fighting they finally evicted the tenants, but what followed was some of the most serious rioting ever seen in the capital. All Metropolitan Police leave was cancelled and officers were drafted in to control the disturbances. MPs attempted to raise the issue for urgent debate in Parliament. A horrified Home Secretary invoked the Public Order Act of 1936 – originally passed to clear Oswald Mosley's fascist Blackshirts off the streets – which gave him draconian powers of detention and arrest.

The St Pancras rent riots, as they were known, became the focus of media and political attention throughout the country. What started as a local row in one part of London had escalated into a dispute of national importance and newsreels buzzed with excitement to take the story across the country. For some, the protesters at the centre of the clashes were working-class heroes fighting for social justice and the 'New Jerusalem' which had been promised by the Labour Government in 1945. But for others the rioters were a symbol of a dangerous radicalism which threatened the very fabric of society and established order.

The story of the St Pancras riots provides a fascinating glimpse into life in post-war Britain. Recovering from the Second World War, the popular image is of a nation relaxing in the living rooms of suburban semis; the children in neatly pressed school uniforms and unwrinkled socks read Enid Blyton, while the adults are being entertained by *Hancock's Half Hour* on the radio. It was an era marked by mass consumerism with the car, the television and the washing machine as the foundation stones of a society in which, boasted the Conservative Prime Minister Harold Macmillan, most people had 'never had it so good.'

But the events in St Pancras reveal a very different side to post-war Britain and the image of a country enjoying the pleasures of warm beer and cricket is a convenient suburban myth. This book follows that story during the post-war period from the end of the Second World War to the election of Harold Wilson as prime minister (1945–64). The heroic stoicism of Londoners during the Blitz is well documented but much less well known is what happened next. After the war, the new society, straining to emerge from the rubble of the war as the 'swinging sixties', had a painful and complicated birth especially in the inner city. The backstory to the riots in St Pancras reveals that this ordinary community in central London – just a mile or so from the Palace of Westminster – struggled to deal with a period of extraordinary economic pressure and turbulent social change.

It is an odyssey of intriguing and exiting political events driven by a colourful, eclectic cast of characters. A frequent condemnation of politics today is that it is a world populated by two-dimensional careerists who know about or understand little else. It is not a criticism that can be levelled at the men and women who provide the cast list of this book. Whatever their human frailties and failings, they belonged to a generation who knew no easy options and whose lives were forged by war (*see* Chapter 9).

If the personalities on the political scene were diverse, there was one single issue that preoccupied ordinary Londoners more than any other at this time – housing. The *Observer* newspaper described many of the homes in St Pancras in the 1950s as 'a national disaster and a national disgrace'. It was a description that could have been applied to plenty of other homes across the capital and the country so that what happened in St Pancras captured national media attention not just because of the violence. The story behind the headlines resonated with readers, viewers and listeners around the capital and beyond because it was their story too.

Nevertheless, the St Pancras riots were rooted in the particular evolution of post-war London and it was here that the battle for decent homes became more difficult than anywhere else. The capital was effectively hollowed out by a frenzy of speculation that transformed the face of the city more profoundly than at any time since the age of Sir Christopher Wren. Offices sprang up where people had once lived and residential property was turned over to commercial use. It was a phenomenon almost unique to London and explains why, compared to other European cities which have vibrant communities living alongside businesses, this is less true in the capital of Britain. The powerful financial lobby argued that their needs were paramount and in the interests of the national economy as a whole. As the price of land in central London soared – and with it the pressure on house building – life for tenants in rented homes became ever more fraught.

It seemed that, in these years, what happened in St Pancras mattered to the rest of the country too and, time and again, local events became national news. Today, London is once again gripped by a housing crisis and much of what happened in St Pancras then seems eerily familiar to us now: a chronic lack of affordable homes in the public sector, sky-high rents and exploitation in the private sector, government ministers who believe that market forces will solve the problem, the failure of planning constraints to rein in the financial sector and a lack of concern for local communities; all these factors have played their part to once again push housing to the top of the political agenda.

One London, Two Nations

The area of central London where many of the events described in this book took place is now part of the London Borough of Camden. In the 1950s the area was covered by the boroughs of Holborn and St Pancras. St Pancras was part of the old county of London and covered an area that included famous names such as Tottenham Court Road, Regent's Park, Camden Town, Kings Cross and St Pancras itself. The local council was generally run by Labour although they lost control to the Tories between 1949–53 and again in 1959–62. At the southern end was the tiny neighbouring borough of Holborn which stretched through parts of Covent Garden almost down to the River Thames. Apart from a brief interlude when it was controlled by Labour (1945–49), Holborn was a solidly conservative council. This was a time when the owners of businesses were allowed to vote twice, once where they lived and again in the district of their business. It was this business vote which returned Tory majorities. The two boroughs had been represented by four parliamentary constituencies until 1950 when boundary changes reduced them to two – Holborn and St Pancras South, and St Pancras North. St Pancras North was always solidly Labour but the south seat was more marginal and Labour lost it to the Tories between 1959 and 1964.

The area was home to bustling finance and commerce which produced fortunes comparable with any other part of London. Yet there was little sign of 'trickle down' and few of the people who lived here shared directly in that wealth. 'There are no millionaires ... but something of almost everything else. In spite of the welfare state, in spite of the fact that nobody now starves, goes in rags or fears the paupers grave, Disraeli's two nations still exist and are strongly represented in this marginal constituency' wrote an *Observer* journalist who covered the 1950 general election campaign in Holborn and St Pancras. 'Somers Town, for strangers to London, is the area from which the great railway expresses start their journeys to the north. People live there. Their back windows may be seen through the smoke from the trains. They all have a voice in this election and join with the prosperous and Lincoln's Inn, and the somewhat less prosperous intellectualism, of Bloomsbury.' A decade later the class divide and stark inequalities of wealth were still a marked feature of the area. A *Daily Star* editorial during the St Pancras riots in the autumn of 1960 described how 'St Pancras is a very mixed area where not all the workers do enjoy the prosperity which everyone takes for granted'.

Family ties were important for many in the neighbourhood. When sociologist Hannah Gavron studied the young wives of St Pancras in 1960–61 she found that more than one in three had been born in the area, four out of ten had parents living within a mile and well over half had sisters living nearby. Seven out of ten, however, said they had no contact with neighbours and a quarter said neither they nor their husband had either family or friends in the area. Alongside this largely stable community a more transient population lived in the large, once prosperous houses which had now been converted into cheap bedsits, small flats and brothels. For some, the experience led to loneliness and isolation: according to coroner's records of the post-war era, Holborn and St Pancras had above average suicide rates compared to many other districts in the capital. Some residents here lived in a twilight world like that brought into view by writers like Lynne Reed Banks in her iconic bestselling novel about London low life, *The L-Shaped Room* (1960). Artists, intellectuals, students, writers and leftist politicians still lived here alongside the artisans and workers in a milieu which another local resident – Charles Dickens – had so memorably described a century before.

'Lively and Quick Tongued'

One of the most visible signs of change in the population was the arrival of the first Commonwealth immigrants who began to arrive in London. In 1948, a change in the law allowed Commonwealth subjects to enter and settle in the UK without restrictions. Compared with the twenty-first century, the numbers who came were very small. It is estimated that there were around 28,000 West Indian/Caribbean and 43,000 Asians (from what are now India, Pakistan or Bangladesh) in the UK in 1950. Over the next decade, immigrants began to arrive in slowly increasing numbers until the Conservative government announced its intention to introduce strict controls in 1961. There was then a surge in new arrivals who wanted to beat the ban – around 16,000 West Indians came to the UK in 1951, a number which leapt to 66,000 in 1961. St Pancras council established a committee to monitor integration and in 1958 it reported that there were 'no signs of discrimination' against new arrivals in the borough. If correct, it was very different from that extended to the West Indian cricketer Leirie Constantine just a decade before. In 1943, Constantine made a reservation for a room at the Imperial Hotel in Russell Square, Holborn but when he tried to check in the booking was annulled. The hotel had a colour bar and Constantine was black. There were no equality laws then but Constantine sued the hotel for breach of contract and won.

The sweltering summer of 1958 did see Britain's first race riots, however, not far from Holborn and St Pancras. The pre-war fascist leader Oswald Mosley's British Union triggered two weeks of street violence, terrorising the West Indian community in Notting Hill. There was obviously work to be done on improving community cohesion. The Gallup polling agency first began to ask questions this time about 'race relations', as they were then known. The general consensus was that they were getting worse, while only 16 per cent of respondents thought that they were improving. Fortunately, the tension did not spread to Holborn and St Pancras to any real extent although some tried to fan the flames and at the 1959 the neo-fascist National Labour Party (NLP) contested the St Pancras North constituency. But apart from publicity when their thugs tried to break up a Labour Party meeting, the NLP had almost no impact and their candidate lost his deposit (*see* Chapter 3).

These new arrivals from the Commonwealth joined other ethnic communities already established in Holborn and

St Pancras. In 1960, one national newspaper described the inhabitants of the area as 'a lively, quick tongued population ... They have many of the East Ender's characteristics but the strong peppering of Greek, Irish and Latin residents gives St Pancras a peculiarly individual tang'. Italian immigrants had settled in large numbers in Holborn at the end of the nineteenth century. Their descendants were still there, worshipping in the Italian Roman Catholic church of St Peter's, or being treated in the Italian Hospital, or drinking and gambling in the Mazzini-Garibaldi club. Further north, along the Euston Road from Kings Cross to Somers Town, lived many Scots and Irish, who had originally come to labour on the railways. They had been in the area for decades and their numbers were continually swelled by new arrivals looking for work in the capital.

One of the largest groups in the area was Greek Cypriot – immigration from the island into the UK increased fourfold between 1960 and 1961. Many of them came to St Pancras or Camden Town and around 1,500 into the Hatton Garden area of Holborn, a significant number in a marginal constituency like Holborn and St Pancras South. As British subjects, with a vote, they were frequently targeted at election times. Edward Crankshaw, one of the *Observer*'s stellar feature writers, reported from the constituency during the 1951 general election campaign. He followed the Tory candidate, Colonel Gluckstein, one of the many former Tory MPs who had lost their seat in 1945 and was bidding to get back to Westminster. Gluckstein, 'observing that 1,500 is more than the last Labour majority, has set out to woo the Cypriots. Canvassers, lacking Modern Greek, find them unassailable, but Tory headquarters has produced a special election address in Greek'. The Holborn and St Pancras South Labour Party, however, were also on the case and they too translated election leaflets into Greek. As local MP from 1953, Lena Jeger cultivated the Cypriot vote assiduously. She took an active interest in the community and raised questions about the Cyprus problem on scores of occasions in the House of Commons. The ex-pat Cypriots and other new arrivals were part of a movement which would subsequently transform the borough, and London, forever and it was an immigrant, the black activist and Caribbean cricket lover CLR James, who perhaps best captured the rich ambience of the district when he wrote 'anyone who lives in this place for any length of time and remains dull need not worry himself. Nothing he will do will ever help him. He was born that way.'

Physically, the area was as varied as its people. Ancient Inns of Court and great centres of learning, such as the British Museum and the University of London, dominated the southern end of the district. The British Museum is now the most visited tourist attraction in London and even then was a renowned centre of world culture and research. The building also housed the British Library – with a reading room underneath a huge dome, larger than that of St Paul's Cathedral – which attracted British and foreign scholars alike; a couple of the many foreign visitors – Marx and Lenin – had spent long hours unravelling the mechanics of capitalism and plotting its inevitable demise here. But some local people would remain barely literate despite spending a life time living in the shadow of the museum. Just to the south was the lively early morning bustle of the Covent Garden fruit and flower market, while immediately to the north were the run-down and slightly seedy streets of old Bloomsbury. The area had famously lent its name to the group of artists and intellectuals that included John Maynard Keynes and Virgina Woolf, who lived here in the 1900s, but many more writers, thinkers, bohemians and oddballs were to be found in the quarter.

The district was dominated by Senate House, centrepiece of the still unfinished University of London. Designed by architect Charles Holden in the 1930s, this awesome art deco building was borrowed by George Orwell for use as the Ministry of Truth in his novel *Nineteen Eighty-Four*. The construction of Senate House destroyed important parts of old Bloomsbury; acres of beautiful Georgian squares and terraces were lost in the 1930s to the university, its institutes and its schools. After the war, when local people lamented the loss of some well-loved building, they were not always clear whether the destruction had been caused by Hitler or the university. The area was also home to the prestigious University College Hospital and some of the most advanced research laboratories in the world, while just a few hundred yards away people died from infections in damp, overcrowded, infested houses or were deformed by their meagre diet.

Along the north of the Euston Road – a more significant divide to local people than any borough boundary – lay the three main rail termini: Euston, St Pancras and King's Cross. These cathedrals of Victorian industry dominated the local economy. The stations, goods yards and warehouses were a major source of jobs, but they came at a price. The noise and smoke pollution from the locomotives was a continual irritant to residents, who complained incessantly about the effects on everything from their laundry to their lungs. Bad as the pollution was, however, residents were frequently tormented by something even worse, and that was the wretched condition of many homes in the area.

'A Gigantic Theft'

In the mid-1920s Father Basil Jellico, a local priest in the Somers Town area at the heart of St Pancras, described his parish as 'really gigantic theft. Overcrowding and poverty here are being used by the Devil in order to steal from the children of God the health and happiness which is their right.' Some improvements were made but forty years later, in 1962, Penguin books published a special report on housing, which singled out Somers Town as still being among the most deprived areas of the capital. In one chapter, architect Eric Lyons wrote passionately about the need for community welfare, saying 'what I want people to do is look beyond the Euston Arch to the slums of St Pancras. When they do that something's bound to happen.' Something did happen, but not what Lyons hoped for. Even as the book went to press the magnificent Euston arch – a national monument built in 1837 at the entrance to the original railway station – was demolished as part of an ugly commercial development. This massive scheme, which completely destroyed the original character of the locality, increased the supply of office space still further without adding a single home (see below). There was a national howl of outrage but it was all too late to save the arch - and the slums remained.

Holborn and St Pancras were, of course, far from isolated examples of poor housing in Britain at the time and the nation's slum houses had been a source of national shame since they were first constructed during the industrial revolution. H. G. Wells wrote angrily that 'It was only because the thing was spread over a hundred years and not concentrated into a few weeks that history fails to realise what a sustained disaster, how much massacre, degeneration and disablement of lives was due to the housing of people in the 19th century.'

While slum housing was recognised as a serious problem before the war, the saturation bombing of British cities during the Second World War simply made a desperate situation intolerable. Nationally, aerial bombing had completely razed over 200,000 homes and another 250,000 were uninhabitable. London had been hard hit and the Blitz took an especially heavy toll in both Holborn and St Pancras. Close to the City and the Thames, Holborn had been pounded during the winter of 1940 and then again by V-weapon (doodlebug) rocket attacks in 1944. The diarist (and later local councillor) Anthony Heap described walking around Holborn one Sunday morning after a raid to discover:

> The whole area has been virtually laid waste ... The best part of Red Lion Street and Eagle Street were burned out. Bedford Row had taken three direct hits and, as a piece de resistance, the whole of Theobalds Road (both sides) ... had been brought to the ground. The casualties must have been enormous.

They were. More than 1,000 people were killed or injured in the raids and one-seventh of all property in the borough was destroyed, including 600 homes. The death toll would have been even worse had around 2,000 people a night not sheltered in Holborn tube station – in defiance of officials whose priority was to keep transport services running. St Pancras did little better. Attracted by the light industry, goods yards and the three main rail termini, Nazi attacks had destroyed 1,600 homes and a lot more property was left badly damaged by the Luftwaffe.

Cleaning up the mess and building new homes was at the top of the political agenda at the end of the war; George VI himself proclaimed, 'The time of destruction is ended, the era of reconstruction begins.' Progress was rapid but the task immense so that well over a decade later novelist Muriel Spark vividly described London streets:

> Buildings in bad repair or no repair at all, bomb sites piled with stony rubble, houses like giant teeth in which decay had been drilled out, leaving only a cavity. Some bomb ripped buildings looked like ancient castles until, at a closer view, the wallpapers of various quite normal rooms would be visible, room after room exposed as on a stage with one wall missing; sometimes a lavatory chain would dangle over nothing from a fourth or fifth floor ceiling; most of all the staircases had survived like some new art form leading up to an unspecified destination that made unusual demands on the mind's eye.

Then, on top of repairing Blitz damage, the demobilisation of troops and the subsequent 'baby boom' added to the pressure: by the late 1940s the crisis threatened to become unmanageable as people moved back into the existing and often squalid housing which remained.

At the general election of 1945 there was cross-party consensus that housing would be a litmus test for the new post-war order. Labour declared that 'housing will be one of the greatest and one of the earliest tests of a Government's real determination' while the Tories argued that 'in the first years of peace the provision of homes will be the greatest domestic task'. The reason for the urgency was visible. The Attlee government (1945–51) made housing a priority and set a national target to provide a 'separate dwelling for every family desiring to have one'. That meant around 750,000 new homes would be needed across the nation. Slum clearance in London and other major cities was essential but far from straightforward because the system was creaking under the demands for other essential construction like schools and hospitals. Everywhere there was a shortage or money, materials and skilled labour.

The new government minister responsible for house building was Aneurin Bevan. Best known as father of the National Health Service (founded in 1948), Bevan was officially Minister for Health and Housing – a combination of roles which recognised the intimate relationship between decent housing and good health. Bevan is rightly praised for the patience and political cunning with which he faced down opponents of his plan for a system of national health. But this was not the limit of Bevan's achievement. He adopted a characteristically audacious approach to housing too and his plans marked a revolutionary change in social policy.

Before the war, the Conservatives had encouraged private builders and speculators to build vast suburban estates for the middle classes. But Bevan now gave 1,700 local authorities sole responsibility for the new house-building programme. It was the biggest single expansion of local government activity in British history. To help the councils with their mammoth task, Bevan arranged for increased subsidies from the Public Works Loans Board, the Treasury body responsible for lending to local authorities. Bevan's scheme allowed local authorities to borrow cheaply from central government and allow them to spread repayment of the loans over several decades. He hoped that local councils in cities like London would provide homes for most people and confidently expected that other options such as renting from the private sector or owner-occupation would diminish as time went on. In addition, Bevan removed the requirement for social housing to be only for the 'working class' because he wanted it provided on the basis of need and his dream was of mixed, integrated communities. As he told the House of Commons in 1946 it was 'part of the housing policy of the Government, to try to prevent the creation after this war, of the kind of villages and housing estates that grew up between the wars, where people of a certain kind of income, were confined together.'

Far from drab uniformity, Bevan harked back to a vision of 'Merrie England' to make his case. 'We want diversified communities, and we are trying to create, in the modern estates, some of the agreeable features of the loveliest villages of England in the seventeenth and eighteenth centuries, where people of different income-groups all lived together almost in the same street. We want to get rid of the "stockbrokers" paradise,' that grew up between the wars.' Bevan now gave local authorities the ability to shape their local communities: 'Therefore, there is no limitation other than the one which the local authority imposes upon itself in the type of house which it provides or the kind of income-group for which it makes provision.' Finally, in a phrase which became famous, Bevan pressed home his idea of a nation which really would be 'all in it together' 'We don't want a country of East Ends and West Ends ... Equally I hope that old people will not live in colonies of their own – they do not want to look out of their windows on an endless procession of the funerals of their friends; they also want to look out on perambulators.'

The New Towns Act (1946) and Town and Country Planning Act (1947) embodied this spirit of mixed communities. Private house building was restricted to one-fifth of the total and Bevan's houses responded to increasingly vociferous popular demands for inside toilets, bathrooms and separate bedrooms. Bevan's houses were larger and better than what came before – or many since. They all had a downstairs toilet, for example, because he intended them to be homes for life and the elderly and the infirm.

Bevan's vision was important. It provided the template both for Labour's housebuilding programme and the framework for party thinking during much of the following decade. In 1951, however, the Tories won the general election and they had very different ideas about how to solve Britain's housing problems. Once Labour left office the Tories concentrated on the number of houses built; it was not until the 1960s that the seminal Parker Morris report (1961) 'Homes for Today and Tomorrow' put the space and amenity of council homes back at the centre of housing policy.

'Houses for the People'

When Winston Churchill became prime minister again in 1951 he appointed Harold Macmillan as the new housing minister with a simple instruction to build 'houses for the people' on an unprecedented scale. And this he did. Macmillan chalked up some impressive totals in his time at the ministry and by 1954 over 350,000 new homes a year were being built. Much of the increase was driven by private sector construction in the new towns or increasing numbers of 'suburban semis' for owner-occupiers. While this was evidently of real benefit to the country it still left a very large number of people who could not afford to buy one of the new homes or who were tied to the city because of their work. This was especially true in inner cities like London. New towns or suburbs were simply not an option for many key workers who were the life blood of the London economy and without whom the metropolis would have ground to a halt. During one Commons debate on housing, the MP for Holborn and St Pancras South, Lena Jeger, invited a Tory housing minister to down to the Covent Garden fruit and flower market so he could 'tell the porters who live in Holborn why they should live in Boreham Wood or Harlow'. 'We have to recognise,' said Jeger, 'that many people are tied to central London ... by their jobs and the vital contribution they make through their work to the community.'

Much of the housing in London remained in a dire condition. Victorian tenements needed bringing up to date (at the very least) and damage from the war repaired. Little of this was being done by private landlords because rents remained pegged at their 1939 level by a statutory wartime control that had never been lifted. It was inevitable that some rents would need to rise but the key questions were by how much and over what time period? The interests of landlords would need to be carefully balanced against the welfare of tenants and in 1954 small rent increases, piecemeal and limited, were allowed to cover essential repair work. This incremental approach recognised the delicate balance of interests and the fragile housing sector in cities like London which were still recovering from the Blitz.

But more sweeping, radical reforms to housing law were soon on the way. In October 1954 Churchill reshuffled his cabinet and the suave, consensual Macmillan was replaced at Housing by the abrasive free marketer, Duncan Sandys. An old Etonian married to Churchill's daughter, Sandys' career nearly came to grief in 1963 when photographs of the Duchess of Argyll performing fellatio on a man whose head was not shown in the camera shot scandalised the country. An enquiry led by Lord Denning managed to (mis)identify the actor Douglas Fairbanks Jr – who had been photographed, masturbating, by the duchess – as the man, and the true identity of the 'headless lover' as Sandys was not confirmed until forty years later. But by then Sandys' political career had taken a back seat to more lucrative connections in the City, although these too carried the whiff of scandal. In the early 1970s, during a furious boardroom battle for control of the giant Lonrho Corporation, it was revealed that $100,000 had been lodged for the chairman, tax free, in a Cayman Island bank account. The chairman was Duncan Sandys. Tory prime minister of the day, Edward Heath, described the scandal as the 'unpleasant and unacceptable face of capitalism' and so Sandys became forever linked with one of the best known phrases in British political history. A fellow – but altogether less sybaritic – right-wing free-marketeer, Enoch Powell, was appointed as Sandys' Parliamentary deputy in 1957.

Sandys and Powell pushed through several pieces of legislation during their time at the ministry between 1954 and 1957, but the objective was always the same: to substitute market forces for local authorities as the main provider of housing. Sandys' policies were a 180-degree reversal of Bevan's ideas, which had made local authorities the key providers of housing. Now, the laws of supply and demand would determine more who got what. The adjustment was so abrupt that it sent a seismic social shock through the London housing market, claiming many victims. The full horror of their position was only fully revealed with the exposé of slum landlords like Perec Rachman during the Profumo Scandal (1963) and documentaries like Ken Loach's classic film about homelessness *Cathy Come Home*, which shook the nation in 1966 (*see* chapter 5).

In the 1950s, tremendous pressure began to build up on all these local communities as it became clear that the post-war plans for London were not being carried through. A monocled professor of civic design, Sir Patrick Abercrombie, had been tasked with the planning of the metropolis but for various reasons – the lack of finance was a major obstacle – his plans were never implemented and the somewhat chaotic, higgledy-piggledy rebuilding of London began almost as soon as the war was over. The capital had, of course, been an important commercial centre and had grown because of this throughout its history. In the past, however, the competing needs of commercial use and residential use had been more finely balanced while in the post-war era, those arguing for affordable homes in the inner cities were, as now, firmly on the back foot.

As a consequence, housing became the issue which dominated the politics of inner London and are areas like Holborn and St Pancras during the post-war era. By the end of the 1940s some 50,000 new homes had been built in London, usually in rather uninspiring but utilitarian blocks, which can still be seen today in the Camden Town and Kentish Town areas of St Pancras. But the increase in supply never remotely kept pace with the pent-up demand. Writing in 1957, St Pancras councillor Clive Jenkins (who later became a well-known white collar trade union leader *see* chapter 9) said that while many of the other policies adopted by the council attracted nationwide interest, it was housing that 'is of most importance to the people of the Borough'. Another local politician, Peggy Duff, agreed that although some of St Pancras' other high-profile policies grabbed headlines, these were peripheral to housing and 'the real battle, the political battle, was over rents'. This was, Duff suggested in her memoirs, 'because housing development was one of the few real powers held by the old Metropolitan Boroughs and certainly housing was the greatest social evil in St Pancras'.

Throughout the post-war period, three powerful drivers worked in London to stifle attempts by councils like St Pancras to alleviate this 'social evil' of sub-standard housing. First and most important was the increasing use of land in central London for commercial rather than residential use. Second was the Conservative insistence on building for owner occupation which was beyond the reach of many people in deprived areas, and finally there was a withdrawal of large scale, institutional landlords from the housing market. These forces were intertwined and need more explanation to make sense of what happened to housing in post-war London.

The Office Boom

'More and more ordinary working people were moved out of the central areas [of London], especially from Holborn where many areas which had once been residential, like those beautiful Holborn terraces ... [were] converted for office use' was how Peggy Duff saw the development of London in the 1950s. The incessant clanking of bulldozers and rumble of cement mixers filled the capital as London became a giant building site after the war. Reconstruction was everywhere but many of the new buildings erected on the sites of buildings damaged or destroyed in the Blitz were for commercial not residential use. Where some people had once lived others were now working, as huge office blocks sprang up around Holborn and southern St Pancras. This was evident even from an early stage of post-war rebuilding and was a soon a source of grumbling. Writing during the general election campaign in 1951, the *Observer* journalist Edward Crankshaw found that Holborners 'still live in homes which are a national disgrace and a national disaster – and see going up around them monumental office blocks, some of them to house the swollen departments of the Governments they elected. They want to know why these things must happen under Labour.'

If the Labour government of 1945–51 had seemed insensitive to local needs in central London, the pace of change became even more marked under the new Tory government (1951–64). In her biography of slum landlord Perec Rachman, Shirley Green summed up what happened next:

> Thanks to the destruction of many office buildings during the blitz, and the fact that post war London was fast becoming an international city, where both British and foreign companies were seeking premises, there was a critical shortage of office accommodation ... but with the arrival of the Tory government in 1951, committed to lifting the restrictions, the way was paved for an office boom which promised enormous returns on capital investment.

Labour saw land as a social good and believed mixed housing produced positive externalities or social benefits in the form of healthy, robust communities. But as the economy began to boom during the 1950s, the clamour for more office space was insatiable and land became just another tradeable commodity. The only way to meet the demand was to offer up more land and buildings which had previously been used for residential use. In the immediate aftermath of the war, much of the potential expansion was thwarted by restrictions on the use of building materials which were scarce and needed for vital public building work, such as schools and hospitals. But with the Conservative Party firmly in control those priorities were about to change and when the government announced the relaxation of building controls in November 1954 there was cheering on the Tory benches in the House of Commons. Where the Labour government had tried to prioritise the building for homes, health and education, the Tories were now more prepared to let market forces dictate what should be built and where.

The Conservative slogan of the day was 'Set the People Free' and one government minister argued that 'the people the government must help are those who do things; the developers whether they are humble or exalted'. In a detailed account of the period, journalist Oliver Marriot concluded the small group most likely to benefit from this laissez-faire approach were indeed humble but there was no better way of handing them exaltation on a plate. The juggernaut of commercial development in London now began to steamroller much in its path. Former editor of the *London Evening Standard* Sir Simon Jenkins wrote that:

> The years 1953–63 were ones in which these men [the developers], supported by the clearing banks and insurance companies were unleashed on the London environment to enjoy a decade of uncriticised and virtually untaxed profiteering. Through their own ingenuity and the inadequacy of those whose duty it was to restrain them, they were able to amass fortunes which must have been beyond their wildest dreams.

Certainly the investors were richly rewarded and the share value of property companies rose by a multiple of eight between 1958 and 1962. Jenkins explained why areas of central London like Holborn and St Pancras changed almost out of recognition in the 1950s and early 1960s.

> An office block could generate rental income in a very short space of time out of all proportion to the cost ... of its site and

construction, so a developer could 'gear up' his assets by borrowing against them for further deals. He could thus expand much faster than an equivalent dealer in any other commodity. With no more than a thousand pounds and a trusting bank manager, a property man in the fifties could become a millionaire in just a few years.

One developer, for example, made a multimillion-pound profit on redeveloping the area around Paddington using just £1,000 of his own money. He was not alone. According to one source, there were some fifty property companies listed on the stock exchange in 1958 (often family affairs) and some 200 by 1960. Speculators began to buzz around the capital. Many remained somewhat shaded characters – one of the biggest, Harry Hyams, was an almost total recluse – but the schemes that they promoted changed the face of London more profoundly than at any time since Sir Christopher Wren after the Great Fire of London in the 1660s.

Astonishingly, no one in Whitehall seemed to be monitoring the impact of the bonanza too closely or how the capital was changing from its pre-war base. In 1959 the St Pancras North MP, Kenneth Robinson, asked in Parliament how much extra office accommodation there would be in central London (beyond the square mile of the City) when all new planned buildings were constructed and what the overall increase would be since 1939. The minister's reply – couched in terms of 'nearest figures', 'estimates' and with 'no precise information' – calculated some 100 million square feet of office space had been built by 1959 and another 15 million would soon be added. But the minister admitted that the government had no idea how much of this was new office space and how much was replacement, and they had no figures at all for 1939.

Almost all of the new development was for business use and the typical property developer in the capital was hardly interested in providing new homes at all because in an open market the richest pickings came not from housing but from the far more lucrative this commercial property market. The social value of a building, let alone aesthetics, was of secondary importance. Around Britain, city centres were gutted to make way for new developments and nowhere was that clearer than in central London. Planning control in inner London was the responsibility of the London County Council (LCC) but too often it seemed that the authority was simply not up to the task of dealing with wily developers. In areas like Holborn and St Pancras mammoth commercial developments, such as that along the Euston Road, destroyed not just the Euston arch (above) but the entire character of the area. The pale blue colouring of the Monopoly board designates the Euston Road as one of London's less profitable areas but in this case the project netted a huge windfall for the constructor: the LCC received land worth £2 million while the developer cleared a £22 million profit on the deal which involved a great deal of stealth and very little public consultation.

Perhaps the most egregious example of post-war development anywhere in London, however, was that of Centre Point in Holborn. In the late 1950s, the London County Council wanted to ease heavy traffic congestion by constructing a roundabout at one end of the world famous Oxford Street. The cash-strapped local authority could not afford to buy the land, and turned to developer Harry Hyams. In return for permission to erect what was then London's tallest skyscraper, the thirty-five-storey Centre Point building, Hyams designed a complex which would allow the roundabout pass underneath the building. Onlookers were stupefied when construction began in 1961; the new building dwarfed every other in the vicinity and destroyed the neighbourhood. The controversy continued for years after completion. Despite the acute shortage of land for either housing or office use, Hyams kept the building empty throughout the 1960s and well into the 1970s and tenants were almost superfluous, partly because, as land prices in London continued to soar, the annual increase in the capital value of the building outstripped the value of any rental income. Construction costs came to £3.5 million, but soon after completion the building was valued at £17 million, netting Hyams a cool £11 million profit. Ironically, the building is only now being converted for residential use – as luxury flats well beyond the budget of most local people. And the roundabout? It was never built and the traffic congestion continued to snarl up the junction.

Incidentally, London's growth as a financial centre was boosted by one final twist which resonates today. In 1958 Sir George Bolton decided to leave his steady job as Deputy Governor of Bank of England to take up the post as Chair of London and South America Bank (BOLSA). A former Tory MP who had lost his seat in 1945, Bolton had a smart idea for expanding the scope and profitability of the financial services sector in London. He developed the Euro-dollar market and the City of London began a new phase of its development – as a global hub for 'off-shore' financial dealings, tax havens and fiscal paradises,

The second driver of policy in the 1950s was the idea that the market rather than the state should be left to solve the problem of poor housing. It was the start of the socially engineered trend toward owner occupation especially evident in the UK and not seen in many other European countries. The Conservatives, who came to power in 1951, shared Labour's view that the need for more new homes was urgent. Housing minister Harold Macmillan described it as 'a national crusade' and, notwithstanding the fact that Macmillan then dropped some of Bevan's requirements for the quality of the houses, built his record as Housing Minister was impressive: more than 680,000 new houses were built in the two years 1953–54. There was, however, a crucial difference in the Tory policy. Where Bevan had encouraged public sector housing, the Conservatives wanted the private sector to provide new homes. By 1954 an increasing number of the new houses being built or renovated were for suburban owner-occupiers, not for city dwellers who wanted to rent. Throughout the 1950s, the Tory central government in Westminster gradually withdrew the financial support from local-authority housing programmes. The result was that as land prices soared, Treasury subsidies to local authorities dwindled. This left councils with ambitious building and regeneration programmes, like St Pancras, trying desperately to bridge an ever-larger gap in funding new building.

The imperative for local councils to step in and fill the housing void was evident too in the population drift away from inner London. New towns like Crawley, Stevenage, Harlow and Hatfield were essential safety valves which often provided better, healthier homes and relieved pressure on inner London's blighted housing. Without doubt, some people left for the gardens and cleaner air in the suburbs. But not all. Market forces and commercial expansion made the provision of decent, affordable housing for those who did stay much harder and this failure could only be remedied by robust local-authority action.

However, suburbanisation could never be a substitute for the thriving inner-city communities that kept the capital functioning. In the fifty years before the Second World War, London had grown rapidly by around 3 million people. After the war the process was reversed and the city began to thin out. Around 1.5 million inhabitants of inner London left the city in the three decades after 1939 and in Holborn and St Pancras the depopulation was clear. The electoral roll in the Holborn and St Pancras South parliamentary constituency, for example, fell from 54,958 in 1950 to 43,272 in 1964 – a drop of 27 per cent. At least part of this depopulation was down to market forces and the increasing cost of decent homes in the city.

The third driver of change was the decline of private landlords during the 1950s. Many small householders gradually stopped taking in lodgers. In some cases increasing wealth meant that they could afford to do without the income from lodgers while in other cases larger houses were subdivided into smaller units and sold. A much more important haemorrhage of rental property occurred when large private, institutional landlords pulled out of the residential to-let property market. The expectation of higher rents from commercial tenants, while rents for residential tenants were pegged to pre-war levels, led several large landlords to exit the market.

Aristocratic and institutional landlords started to divest themselves of their extensive residential estates in post-war London. Rents had been pegged, the individual properties were expensive to maintain, and prostitution was rife. The Church Commissioners, responsible for the management of large property portfolio in Paddington for example, were distressed to hear themselves described as 'the biggest brothel owners in Europe'. The Commissioners sold off vast chunks of their Paddington estate in 1955 and 1958, reducing their residential holdings from over 40,000 to units to just 4,000. And the same was happening across London. St Pancras when the council acquired the Camden estate of some 400 run-down flats in desperate need of repair from the Church Commissioners.

'The Growing Evil of Land Speculation'

The Holborn and St Pancras South Constituency Labour Party (CLP) perfectly understood the reasons behind the housing crisis in the capital. Minutes of meetings from the time show that it was a continual topic of discussion in the party. In the mid-1950s it called on the London County Council (LCC) to revise the original Abercrombie Plan for London and sought a new investigation into London's problems to examine 'traffic flow, housing integrated communities and the limitation of office building'. The Holborn and St Pancras party also suggested that the LCC examine the adequacy of existing powers for taking land into public ownership. Again, in 1959 the Holborn and St Pancras South CLP called on the LCC to restrict office building, encourage the repopulation of central London and ensure that further development was by 'public authorities and not by private speculation.' The following year, 1960, the CLP selected yet another resolution on housing to submit for debate at the annual, national Labour Party conference:

> This conference condemns the growing evil of land speculation, particularly in building sites; this results in gross distortion of planning, the imposition of crippling burdens on public authorities which need land for housing, schools and hospitals, roads and other social purposes; and causes impossible unfair rents and purchase prices for those in need of homes. Conference therefore instructs the NEC to investigate the position urgently with a view to formulating a policy statement which will provide for the nationalisation of both urban land and hitherto undeveloped land on which it is intended to build, together with an interim emergency scheme of price control.

And so it went on. Local Labour Party activists, like so many others in central London at the time, could see what was going on around them. They understood that the forces of market capitalism were creating housing havoc in central London and they attempted to push back against the tide. It was a conflict of ideas that would end in a collision which had national repercussions. In the 1950s the housing policy under the Labour administration on St Pancras council was based on an ambitious building programme combined with low, affordable rents. Then, in 1959, Labour lost control of the council to the Conservatives who slashed the building programme and pushed through stiff rent increases. It was this abrupt U-turn in the housing policy that triggered a catatonic reaction among the tenants, leading to forced evictions, a rent strike and some of the most serious rioting in Britain since the 1930s.

None of this would have happened, however, without the very singular politics of the area in the post-war epoch. The battle for decent housing was one waged across the capital in the 1950s and 1960s but it assumed a particular form in St Pancras for various reasons. Chapter 2 explains how bitter divisions in the Labour Party were worked through in Holborn and St Pancras with disastrous consequences for the left. Chapter 3 describes how various policies adopted by the council gave it a national profile unequalled by any other local authority; one of these contributed to Holborn and St Pancras becoming the birthplace of the biggest protest movement in post war British history – the Campaign for Nuclear Disarmament (CND) – and is the subject of Chapter 4. These chapters are essential to understand the febrile context of the housing conflicts and the rent riots – the focus of this book, and the subjects of chapters 5–8.

Chapter 2

THE MYSTERIOUS MR LAWRENCE

So long as there is exploitation in society the workers will kick against it – that is the highest moral. All the rest is cant, humbug and hypocrisy.

John Lawrence, leader of St Pancras council

In the first decade of the twentieth century, expatriate Russians were attracted to the Holborn and St Pancras district of London like iron filings to a magnet. These were not, as now, oligarchs looking to snap up investment bargains in London's buoyant property market but down-at-heel revolutionaries who had fled the country after the failed attempts to overthrow Tsar Nicholas II. One frequent visitor to the area was Vladimir Lenin. In 1902 he met another émigré, Leon Trotsky, for the first time at his lodgings just off the Grays Inn Road which runs between Holborn and St Pancras – much of their mass propaganda was published from various addresses in the district – and in the spring of 1908 Lenin lodged at No. 21 Tavistock Place in Bloomsbury. Fifty years later, the politics of the two revolutionaries surfaced again in Holborn and St Pancras. A small group of Trotskyist sympathisers known as 'entryists' joined the local Labour Party and one of their number, John Lawrence, became leader of the St Pancras council. Lawrence emerged as a figure of national importance in the Labour Party of the 1950s but his story remains incomplete. Despite repeated Freedom of Information requests, the government refuses to release intelligence that the security services undoubtedly collected on Lawrence and his associates. Nevertheless, this chapter explains what is known about the man, his group and the context in which they came to dominate the politics of St Pancras.

The Lab-Con Years

Post-war Britain was very much a two-party, Labour-Conservative state. At the general election of 1951, for example, nine out of ten voters opted either for Labour or the Tories. Other parties – Communists, Liberals and Independents – were represented but this was as a result of local peculiarities and their influence, like their numbers, was marginal. Following the general election of July 1945, the Labour Party swept to power with a 145-seat majority and Clement Attlee became prime minister. The Second World War was still not quite over, but expectations were high. Labour's visionary manifesto offered radical economic and social reform – 'a new Jerusalem' – which chimed with the popular mood. Legislation came thick and fast. Loss-making but vital industries like coal, electricity, gas and railways were nationalised, the welfare state was beefed up and a universal, free at the point of use National Health Service was launched. In modern political parlance, Labour set about fixing holes in the roof caused by the neglect of the Tory-dominated inter-war years and the destruction of the Second World War. But none of this massive effort to modernise Britain was achieved while the sun shone. The war and its aftermath left Britain on the verge of bankruptcy – the diaries of Chancellor of the Exchequer Hugh Dalton record how he lay awake at night calculating exactly how many days (not weeks or months) were left until the country actually ran out of foreign exchange.

By 1950, the important social reforms were not enough; continued rationing, austerity, and a brutal devaluation of sterling wore away at public support for the government. At the general election of 1950, the Labour majority in the House of Commons evaporated to just five. The government limped on for another year before Attlee called a second general election in 1951. Despite Labour polling nearly 14 million votes – the largest number for any British political party in the twentieth century – the Tories won by a majority of seventeen. When Churchill returned to Downing Street in 1951 he was about to enter his seventy-seventh year. Although he was ailing physically, the old man was politically unassailable. Several younger colleagues fancied a crack at getting the top job, but to their frustration Churchill clung to office, despite suffering from a couple of strokes, news of which was kept from the public. Churchill's primary purpose during his second term was to try and direct the Cold War; foreign policy had a very high profile at this time and it was a role for which he felt himself to be uniquely, indispensably qualified (*see* Chapter 4). Churchill was far less interested in domestic policies such as housing and was content to leave this and most national issues to other ministers, as he had done during the war (*see* chapters 5–7).

Churchill finally resigned in the spring of 1955 and his successor, Sir Anthony Eden, called a snap election almost immediately. In the context of robust economic growth and a hopelessly divided Labour opposition, the Tories consolidated their dominance of Westminster with an increased majority of sixty. After years of waiting for the much coveted premiership, Eden looked to be the right man at the right time but few political careers have crashed quite so quickly or so spectacularly. Late in 1956, the Egyptians took control of the Suez Canal and Eden's bungled response brought his premiership to an abrupt end. The international humiliation was so profound that an entire generation of British politicians, commentators and diplomats came to shudder at the mere mention of the word 'Suez'. It was left to Harold Macmillan to pick up the pieces when, against the odds, he became prime minister in 1957. Macmillan projected the image of a patrician Tory to calm the post-Suez jitters, engineer an economic boom, and restore Tory fortunes. At the general election of 1959 the Conservatives increased their majority to 100 and Macmillan earned the sobriquet 'Supermac'. But from this highpoint, Tory popularity began to slide in the early 1960s. The economy turned sour and the government became mired in a series of sensational, damaging scandals: the Vassall spy case, the Profumo affair and the Rachman exposes to name but three.

Apparently under the (mistaken) impression that he was about to die, Macmillan hastily resigned the premiership in 1963 and was succeeded by the aristocratic Alex Douglas-Home. It turned out to be a poor choice for the Tories. Whereas the old Etonian Macmillan had seemed blithely reassuring in 1957, Britain had moved on by 1964. Many people saw Douglas-Home as a rather dunder-headed anachronism whose understanding of economics was, by his own confession, based on exercises with matchsticks. Against Labour's new young leader Harold Wilson, a smart northern grammar school boy-cum-Oxford don, there was only going to be one winner; at the general election of 1964 Wilson became prime minister – head of the first Labour government for thirteen years.

Bevan and the Bevanites

While the Conservatives were the party of national government between 1951 and 1964, Labour embarked on a period of internal civil war in opposition. After the general election defeat of 1951 the party was dispirited and exhausted. Leaders like Clement Attlee and Herbert Morrison, who played key roles defeating Nazism and then reconfiguring Britain after 1945, were burned out by the strain of an extraordinary decade in high office. Another giant of the Labour movement, Ernest Bevin, died in the spring of 1951 and left a gap that nobody else could fill. Labour needed to regenerate and find a new direction: but where to? And what was the party now for? The party's national agent at the time described Labour's aims as 'the use of constitutional means to achieve socialism'. But that kind of vague formulation begged as many questions as answers and Labour became consumed by an increasingly acrimonious, self-destructive debate about its future purpose and split, crudely, into three different factions from left to right. On the left, the 'Bevanites' demanded that Labour adopt a more full-on socialist agenda. On the right, the consolidationists tended to be older party figures who were primarily interested in defending the advances of the 1945–51 Attlee government. And in the centre were the revisionists, led by future leader Hugh Gaitskell, who sought to devise a fresh programme for the party which would take account of economic and social change.

In the dying days of office, the Labour government was rocked by the resignations of three senior ministers. By far the most important departure was that of Aneurin ('Nye') Bevan, the youngest member of Attlee's Cabinet who had piloted the launch of the NHS. He was, without question, the most charismatic Labour politician of his generation and his influence on the Labour Party in the 1950s was immense. Jean Mann, a Scottish Labour MP in the 1950s and one of the few women in the House of Commons, was by no means a supporter of Bevan. She was, nevertheless in awe of the Welshman and compared him to Churchill. 'No politician of my age could escape Churchill,' she recalled, 'The only one who could match him in debate was Aneurin Bevan ... and when Mr Churchill entered the House he always looked across to see if Bevan was in his seat. And then battle began.' Former Tory MP Jonathan Aitken remembered a youthful trip to the House of Commons where his father was also a Conservative MP. When he was introduced to a very aged Winston Churchill, Aitken expressed his ambition to be a great orator like the old Tory leader. 'I'm not an orator,' growled Churchill, 'I just read my speeches. The only real orator in this place is Aneurin Bevan.'

Yet Bevan was also an enormously divisive figure in the party and in the spring of 1951 he resigned from the government in protest against the introduction of some charges to the NHS.

The rights and wrongs of Bevan's argument have been debated ever since but what all sides agree on is that the move had disastrous consequences for Labour. In the words of one Bevan biographer, it 'opened a Pandora's box of grievances, mutual suspicion and genuine differences of political philosophy which, once released, proved impossible to put back in the box again ... on the contrary, [they] took wing and multiplied to create a deep division in the Labour Party'. It was in the context of the confusion brought about by these splits and schisms that the Trotskyist entryists began to take control of the Labour Party in Holborn and St Pancras.

The revisionists in the centre wanted to modernise the Labour Party. They argued that the reforms of the Attlee government had built a new social and economic equilibrium which needed to be recognised and accommodated by the party. The most sophisticated revisionist thinker was Tony Crosland, a bohemian, cigar-smoking Oxford don who later became foreign secretary. In 1956, Crosland published a highly influential book called *The Future of Socialism* in which he asked, 'Does it make sense to go on speaking as though contemporary Britain were still similar in kind to the society historically designated by the word capitalism? Surely not.' Crosland believed that the party's commitment to wholesale nationalisation dictated by Clause IV of its constitution (written in 1918) was long out of date. He tried to construct a new narrative to explain the increasingly fluid social order, embrace the mixed economy and produce policies that would help Labour cut more easily across class barriers – or, as Labour strategists would now say, get beyond its core vote.

But Crosland's attempt to update established thinking did not chime with many of Labour's grass-roots activists; when party leader Hugh Gaitskell later tried to encapsulate them in a updated Clause IV he was firmly rebuffed by a wave of opposition within the party. The Labour activists' champion was Nye Bevan, with his emphasis on traditional socialist values. Bevan argued that despite Labour's achievements between 1945 and 1951, a greater redistribution of wealth did not mean that the working class had not gone away. On the contrary, it was a group with distinct values and aspirations that Labour needed to reflect. Bevan argued that the party required a bolder socialist programme to motivate the working class, not dilute its fundamental principles in an attempt to appeal to other social groups. Bevan himself was firmly rooted in traditional working-class values and he promoted a distinctly core-vote strategy. He wrote warmly of his constituency as 'the district which was the cradle of heavy industry in Britain - Ebbw Vale, Tredegar, Dowlais, Merthyr Tydfil, Rhymmeny - all these names are familiar to students of the industrial revolution'.

Bevan's emotional reverence for his own roots and their place in British history was clarified intellectually by the study of Marxist theory. He readily acknowledged the influence of rationalist Marx but even when doing so could not resist using the language of a south Wales baptist:

> In so far as I can be said to have had any training at all, it has been in Marxism ... Nor was I alone in this. My experience has been shared by thousands of young men and women of the working class of Britain. The relevance of what we were reading to our own industrial and political experience had all the impact of divine revelation. Everything fell into place. The dark places were lighted up and the difficult ways made easy.

Bevan was no crude Marxist, but he continued to believe in the contradictory interests of economic class and was quick to reject ideas of converging social interests, which revisionists like Crossland were trying to find. Bevan was enormously popular among grass-roots activists and Bevanism quickly became a conduit for various frustrations: with the Attlee government, with the disappointment of election defeats in 1950 and 1951 and with the drift of policy toward the centre. But he offered no real worked-out alternative. He articulated – brilliantly – a traditional message that was easier to grasp than the more arid, if intellectually rigorous, approach of Crossland's revisionism. But if revisionism seemed to have substance without popular appeal, Bevanism had popular appeal but lacked substance. It was often difficult to see of what exactly Bevanism sought to do or how it was relevant to some of the rapid social changes taking place in the post-war era. It is something of a mystery that a man who was so flexibly creative in office became so inflexibly destructive in opposition. Bevanism became something of a distraction rather than driver of change and there were two main reasons why it failed: the first was political, the second organisational.

Politically, Bevanism lacked cohesion even among the inner caucus at Westminster. In late 1952, party leader Clement Attlee warned that the Bevanites were 'a party within a party with a separate leadership, separate meetings, with its own press'. Seen from the inside, however, it looked rather different. A leading Bevanite MP and later cabinet minister, Richard Crossman, mused in his diary:

> What a mysterious thing the Left is. Why is this person Left and that person Right? What binds the Group together? In our case, there is the old Keep Left Group who did work out a certain homogeneity, with superimposed on it Nye Bevan and Harold Wilson, who have almost nothing in common, and a number of their personal supporters...who, as far as I can see, have no coherent political attitude.

Despite long discussions over lunches and dinners, the group had difficulties in producing clearly defined aims. According to Crossman, the Bevanites found it hard to make decisions about policy or strategy:

> The Group, indeed, was a bit scared of facing facts for fear of finding the problems insoluble. Of course it may well be that the problems are insoluble – this is a type of philosophic fatalism

which I find acceptable enough [Crossman was another Oxford don] but which Nye, as a sensible politician, instinctively rejects ... A certain amount of utopianism is essential. The question is whether you can control it and keep it within reasonable bounds.

The endless talk over good food and fine wine in the Commons or at Crossman's house in Westminster simply failed to come up with concrete policies or define what 'essential utopianism' really meant, let alone keep it 'within reasonable grounds'. Some contemporary commentators have been more critical and Labour historian Professor David Howell concluded that 'the Labour left in the early fifties remained in the thrall of two ghosts - an emotional traditionalism, and a Stalinism whose intolerance and rigidities were perceived even by the previously sympathetic. The old gods had failed the left – the intellectual poverty of Bevanism reflected in part this barren heritage'.

This failure to define a coherent political purpose led to a second problem – organising Bevanite dissent. Bevan was frequently accused of organising a 'party within a party', which would have been grounds for his expulsion from Labour. But to the frustration of people around him nothing could have been further from the truth. One leading Bevanite MP Ian Mikardo remembered that Bevan reacted strongly against organising support within the Labour Party and in his diary Crossman explains that 'Nye is an individualist ... He dominates discussion simply because he is fertile in ideas but leadership and organisation are things that he shrinks away from'. There was occasional talk of taking control of some constituency parties to de-select anti-Bevanite MPs. But the low-level grumbling about particular MPs was without any real impetus and in any event was firmly resisted by the party's National Executive Committee (NEC).

In a particularly despairing diary entry, Crossman lamented that the twin failures of policy and organisation went hand in hand so that 'the fact is that Bevanism and the Bevanites seem much more important, well organised and Machiavellian to the rest of the Labour Party than they do to us who are in the Group and who know that we are not organised, that Aneurin can never be persuaded to have any consistent ... strategy and that we have not even got to the beginning of a coherent, constructive policy'. Bevan's resignation triggered what turned out to be along running civil war within Labour. Between 1951 and 1955, party members seemed to spend more time fighting with each other than offering any potent opposition to the Tories. By 1955, after four years of incessant, visceral argument between the Labour's competing factions, the Bevanite challenge seemed to have run its course. The crunch came in December that year when Hugh Gaitskell, standard-bearer of the revisionist modernisers, trounced Bevan in the election for the leadership of the Labour Party.

From then on began a slow, painful process of rapprochement between the different sections of the party. The Tories had just won a general election with an increased majority and wounds, both personal and political, needed to be healed. In 1956 Bevan accepted Gaitskell's invitation to return to the leadership of the Labour Party and quietly acquiesced to the new direction of the party. The two of them worked effectively together during the Suez crisis to unseat Prime Minister Anthony Eden – Gaitskell turned in a memorable Commons performance while in Trafalgar Square Bevan made one of his finest ever speeches. In the autumn of 1957, Bevan further discombobulated his erstwhile supporters by turning on them with a fiery speech in favour of nuclear weapons at the Labour Party conference (*see* Chapter 4). Thereafter, recognising that unity would be a precondition for success at the next general election, both Gaitskell and Bevan seemed increasingly prepared to swallow their differences – and to persuade their followers to do likewise.

When the Labour leadership closed ranks around a more centrist strategy, some party activists were dismayed and nowhere was this more evident than in St Pancras. Like many others, the

Holborn and St Pancras South Labour Party was solidly Bevanite and both Dr Santo Jeger and then Lena Jeger, the local MPs, were allies of Bevan in parliament. After 1956 both the local Labour Party and St Pancras council continued to march resolutely to the sound of the Bevanite drum – and now at an increasing pace. Successful political strategies frequently rely on good timing – policies are most effective when they catch the popular mood. Unfortunately for St Pancras Council, their timing was out and one of the main reasons for the subsequent debacle was the failure of the local Labour Party to keep in step with the national leadership.

Bevanism's failure to do more than provide mood music meant that others could sequester the energy of the Bevanite movement for their own ends. And that is precisely what happened in St Pancras. Where Bevanism was imprecise, John Lawrence appeared to be very clear about his political direction, and his identification with the Bevanite tendency added to credibility. He was rumoured to be a personal friend of Nye Bevan and Barbara Castle, although this was an exaggeration according to the latter. Nevertheless, press comment that Lawrence's aspirations were 'pinned to the Bevanite star' was certainly true: Bevanism provided the national political context for John Lawrence and his group in St Pancras.

So who was John Lawrence? He is scarcely known in Camden today. His name cannot be found anywhere in the town hall of the council which he came to lead and the security services keep his file firmly shut from the public gaze. Yet in the 1950s Lawrence was an important figure on the left and from what we do know it is possible to put together a picture of a man whose political influence went far beyond St Pancras or even London. Disgusted with the misery and squalor of the Great Depression in the 1930s, John Lawrence, like many of his generation, joined the Communist Party. When Stalin entered into a pact with Hitler, Lawrence became disillusioned and moved into the chaotic world of Trotskyist politics where factions split, reformed and then split again with vertiginous speed. For a while Lawrence was a paid organiser of the Revolutionary Communist Party (RCP) which he joined, resigned from and rejoined again. Then in late 1947, Lawrence was one of a small group of Trotskyists who joined the Labour Party in St Pancras as what is known as an 'entryist'. Entryism is a strategy based on the instructions of Leon Trotsky who, before being murdered by a Stalinist agent, had at times instructed his supporters to join (enter) social democratic parties and ginger them into becoming revolutionary organisations. With the Labour landslide of 1945 there was little room for other parties of the left, let alone the usual mantra of 'betrayal of the working class' and the RCP went into swift decline.

Lawrence climbed aboard the Labour bandwagon and as the years went on found kindred spirits on the Labour left who were dispirited by what they felt was the slow pace of change. Looking back now, the Attlee government of 1945–51 is often seen as one of mould-breaking reform. But that is not how it seemed to everyone at the time. The Attlee government was subjected to sustained criticism by the party's left wing, led by the 'Keep Left' group of Labour MPs in Westminster, including Michael Foot and Nye Bevan's wife Jennie Lee. Many of the critics later became leading Bevanites.

Socialist Outlook, Socialist Fellowship and John Lawrence

In late 1948, Lawrence began to edit a new weekly magazine called *Socialist Outlook* which he founded with fellow RCP entryist and veteran British Trotskyist Gerry Healy (Healy had previously run a magazine called *Militant*). The primary purpose of the *Socialist Outlook* was to ease the entrists integration with the mainstream Labour left. The paper was financed by the successful architect and sixty-one-year-old Labour MP for Mitcham Tom Braddock, who also provided the print shop. The editorial board included entrists living in St Pancras, a trade union leader and Braddock.

In the first edition, Lawrence explained what the *Socialist Outlook* was about. He insisted that the Conservatives could be routed in 1950 'if the Labour Party comes before the electorate with a clearly defined programme which rejects all compromise with rotten capitalism. *Socialist Outlook* intends to play a practical part in helping achieve such a Labour victory by reasserting and fighting for the basic beliefs of Socialism'.

Tom Braddock gave the new magazine a breathless thumbs-up: 'Welcome to the *Socialist Outlook*,' he wrote, 'it may be in time. It is now certain that the British Labour Party's attempt to achieve socialism in this country by compromise and gradual methods is going to fail. This is no fault of socialism or the Labour Party itself. The attempt had to be made, our people being what they are, and having had the Fabian Society talking to them for so many years. No party could have gained power in 1945 on any other terms. Other methods will now have to be adopted.' Quite what these 'other methods' would be was not spelled out but it was evident that *Socialist Outlook*'s whole approach to radical politics was far more hard-edged than that of the mainstream Labour Party. This was confirmed in a subsequent editorial by John Lawrence, which provided an important insight into his politics:

> So long as there is exploitation in our society, so long will the workers kick against it and continue to demand an end to it. ... the workers will continue to insist that society be organised in such a way that the wealth belongs to those who have created it. And that, until we have finished with capitalism, is the highest moral. All the rest is cant, humbug and hypocrisy.

As would become evident, Lawrence's dismissal of any political compromise as 'cant, humbug and hypocrisy' continued to be his organising principle when he was the Leader of St Pancras Council.

The differences between *Socialist Outlook* and orthodox Labour thinking went beyond mere differences of policy, important though those disagreements were. The paper frequently seemed to suggest that liberal democracy could be bypassed by extra-parliamentary mass movements as the way forward to a socialist society. *Socialist Outlook* was prepared to countenance quasi-revolutionary politics inside a party which was not. That much was clear from the foundation of the Labour Party. In 1918 Labour adopted a constitution that created individual members for the first time. The constitution pledged the party to socialism but rejected the revolutionary methods of the Russian Bolsheviks. Labour was committed to liberal democracy and working within the British parliamentary system. The Communist Party's attempts to affiliate to Labour throughout the 1920s were repeatedly rejected by votes at Labour's annual conference. By the end of the decade the CP gave up because the Soviet Comintern now decided that democratic socialist parties were in fact 'social fascists', enemies of the people, and that good communists should have nothing to do with them. When the line from Moscow changed again in the mid-1930s there were renewed demands for a 'Popular Front' in which communists, socialists and others would organise jointly against fascism. Labour remained wary. In 1930 the party published a *List of Proscribed Organisations*, membership of which was held to incompatible with membership of the Labour Party. The list expanded in the 1930s to include a number of 'front organisations' being used by communists to link in with, and so influence, the Labour Party. Proscribing whole organisations dealt with the problem of communist influence on one level but it was much harder to prevent individuals or groups of individuals – whether communist or Trotskyist – from clandestinely joining the Labour Party. And this is what John Lawrence did.

Socialist Outlook provided a vehicle for Lawrence's beliefs and propaganda; it now needed an organisation to agitate for more left-wing polities within the Labour Party. A new network called Socialist Fellowship (SF) was established and directed by an executive that included several Labour MPs (Ellis Smith, Fenner

Brockway, Tom Braddock, and Ron Chamberlain) and, of course, John Lawrence. The mission statement outlined some general principles and suggested a level of commitment appropriate to a religious sect.

> The Socialist Fellowship is an association of Labour Party members pledged to work for an early attainment of a socialist society. It expects members to give practical proof of their devotion to socialism by sustained activity within their Labour, Trade Union or Co-operative organisations. It advocates socialisation, workers control, ending the gross inequalities of income, a socialist Europe and freedom for the colonies.

The organisation was ambitious. The co-ordinators envisaged that within eighteen months the SF would have some 30,000 members across the country and funds of £1,000. Lawrence threw himself into the organisation of events with characteristic zeal. During the general election campaign of 1950, for example, *Socialist Outlook* and Socialist Fellowship jointly organised a Great Socialist Demonstration at St Pancras town hall. A jazz band and choir were on hand to liven up the event for a team of speakers, which included six Labour MPs and John Lawrence. If the ideological content was pure, the razzmatazz of the transmission was on the most popular level possible. This populist touch was a recurring feature of Lawrence's political style in later years at the same town hall.

Socialist Fellowship had to proceed with care, however, because under the Labour Party rules it was forbidden to form a 'party within a party'; if the SF were added to Labour's list of Proscribed Organisations it would be effectively stymied. Fenner Brockway (whose statue stands in Red Lion Square in Holborn) knew this only too well. He had been the leader of the radical left Independent Labour Party (ILP), which had decided to split from the Labour Party in 1932. The ILP wanted a more urgent, red-blooded socialist programme. Nye Bevan described the breakaway group as 'pure but impotent', and so it proved. The ILP became a marginal, irrelevant force in British politics and was dwarfed by the Labour Party. Brockway rejoined Labour and was determined not to make the same mistake again. At the inaugural SF conference, he told delegates that 'If we are to succeed where the ILP failed we must remember we are first and foremost members of the Labour Party desirous of serving it. Membership of the Socialist Fellowship must mean not less work for the Labour Party but more.'

Before the general election in 1950, *Socialist Outlook* had been openly critical of what it saw as the timidity of Labour's policies. Lawrence dismissed the socialist rhetoric of the party's draft manifesto, *Labour Believes in Britain* (1949), as 'ritualistic curtseys to the movement's founders which are clearly not meant to be taken seriously'. When Labour suffered a crushing comedown in the 1950 general election many took that as a sign that the electorate were tiring of Labour's approach to government and were looking for a change. John Lawrence took the opposite view. He argued that Labour's failure in the 1950 general election was due to the party's lack of credibility among the electorate as serious, socialist challengers to the Conservatives and that the Socialist Fellowship was needed now more than ever. There was certainly plenty of support for this analysis among a hard core of Labour activists; by 1950 Socialist Fellowship was expanding rapidly and *Socialist Outlook* went from a monthly to weekly publication.

But then came a development that split the SF and put an end to the movement. On 25 June 1950, communist forces from North Korea invaded South Korea. The aggression was swiftly condemned by the United Nations Security Council, which agreed a plan for military intervention – including the use of British troops. The most important effect of the Korean War on the Labour left was Nye Bevan's resignation when NHS charges were levied to pay for the cost of military action (see above). But the conflict also challenged the unity of the *Socialist Outlook* and Socialist Fellowship. MPs Brockway and Smith backed their own front bench and intervention in Korea in the House of Commons – they were, after all, Labour MPs. John Lawrence disagreed. He furiously denounced the government's action as 'imperialist' and described the MPs' acquiescence as 'pathetic'. Not surprisingly, both Smith and Brockway immediately resigned from *Socialist Outlook*'s steering committee.

For the next few months *Socialist Outlook* continued to attack the Labour government at every turn and promoted a platform of what it called 'a 100 per cent socialist democracy' with the implication that this differed from the compromises demanded by liberal democracy. By the spring of 1951, the Labour Party's National Executive Committee (NEC) had seen enough. It decided that even the most stretched imagination could no longer regard the SF as working for the Labour Party. The NEC ruled that the Socialist Fellowship was now advocating a separate programme from Labour and banned party members from having anything further to do with the organisation. This was a serious blow for the entryists. But, just at the moment when they might have become outcasts from Labour, the birth of Bevanism suddenly boosted their standing in the party.

Nye Bevan's resignation from the government in April 1951 in protest against the introduction of NHS charges was a profound shock that suddenly created a huge new force field in Labour politics. John Lawrence and Gerry Healy were quick to grasp the implications. They argued that Bevanism was a new 'centrism' within the Party which must be exploited. *Socialist Outlook* ran headlines that screamed support for Bevan: 'Fight Toryism in Labours ranks! Defend the health service! Build the left wing!' The journal willingly seized the opportunity to support Bevan – but as a figurehead, not as a leader. Lawrence argued that Bevanism was 'a further demonstration of deep conflict developing within the Labour movement ... the party is rapidly dividing into right and left'.

John Lawrence's revolutionary politics were neatly embedded in the Bevanite surge but he was still an object of suspicion. In 1953 he was selected by Woodford Labour Party to be their parliamentary candidate at the next general election. Alarm bells rang in Transport House, the Labour Party's HQ in Westminster. Woodford was Prime Minister Winston Churchill's seat and whoever the Labour candidate was, they would inevitably be in the media spotlight. The Labour chiefs in Transport House did not want that person to be Lawrence. They called him in for an interview and when he gave 'unsatisfactory replies' to their questions about Labour policy they struck out his candidature. He continued to edit *Socialist Outlook* but it was eclipsed by another magazine, *Tribune,* which had more influential contributors and spawned a national network; given that Bevan had been the founding editor of *Tribune* before the war it was not surprising that it should become the in-house paper for the Bevanites. *Socialist Outlook* finally folded after internal feuding on the editorial board about the next big row to rock the Labour Party – German rearmament.

From today's perspective, the largely forgotten argument about German rearmament after the Second World War looks peripheral, even trifling. But in the early 1950s it was a huge issue, debated with passion and was a source of yet more splintering on the left. By 1954 the Americans were encouraging West Germany to rearm as a further bulwark against Soviet expansionism in central and western Europe (West Germany became part of NATO in early 1955). The policy was supported by the Churchill government and some sections of the Labour Party. Others in Labour opposed German rearmament for a variety of reasons. The aged Hugh Dalton, a leading light in the Attlee government, could not get over two world wars and told some of his prodigies that the 'Germans were murderers, individuals excepted. They'd killed all my friends in the First war... 'Deutschland Über Alles' was their song and they meant it.' Others in the Labour Party were pacifists and opposed any escalation of the cold war. Nye Bevan was one objector and in April 1954 he resigned – again – from the Labour front bench.

Socialist Outlook sped to Bevan's defence with a front-page headline proclaiming 'Left Unity is the Next Step'. Ironically, it was to be one of the last headlines the paper ever ran because unity was in short supply even on the editorial board. Although board members agreed on their opposition to German rearmament, they were bitterly divided about why they were opposed. John Lawrence was neither a German-hater nor a pacifist but opposed rearmament because of the threat which it might pose to the Soviet Union, insisting, 'anti-communism, anti-Russianism – that is today's trap for the workers'. For someone who had spent a decade in Trotsyist politics, this defence of the Stalinist USSR was a startling departure from orthodoxy. His erstwhile comrades were enraged. Lawrence was accused of drifting toward Stalinism, the Trotskysts' original sin, and sacked as editor *Socialist Outlook* in May 1954. As if that schism were not damaging enough, the *coup de grâce* was then delivered by Labour's NEC, which proscribed the journal and expelled Gerry Healy in the summer of 1954. Bevan remained a supporter.

'I suppose that I shall be banned for this' said a smiling Nye Bevan as he bought one of the final editions of *Socialist Outlook*. Lawrence put the photo on the 1954 Labour conference edition of the paper. *Naïve* or still confused about paper's primary purpose, leading Bevanites rallied to defend the journal threatened with closure. Bevan's wife, Jennie Lee MP, then contributed an article for the final edition headlined 'Socialist Outlook does have the right to make a contribution'.

At a meeting of 300 people to defend the journal at Holborn Hall, Michael Foot claimed that if the NEC got away with the proscription of *Socialist Outlook*, 'they will look round for the next one on the list' (i.e. *Tribune* of which he, Foot, was a former editor). Foot also penned an intemperate article for *Tribune* in defence of *Socialist Outlook*. Under the headline 'I Call This an Outrage' he wrote:

> For the first time in its history, so far as I am aware, the leaders of the Labour Party have taken steps to suppress a newspaper. Such a decree might fittingly be issued within a fascist or Communist Party. That it should be issued by leaders of a democratic party is an outrage. The good name of the Labour Party requires that this stupid, cowardly and totalitarian edict should be rescinded.

These were powerful words and ones which came back to haunt him. In 1982, with Foot as leader, Labour's National Executive Committee moved to ban the Trotskyist paper *Militant* and Foot's words from thirty years before appeared again and again on the paper's front page.

Why Labour chiefs on the NEC did not expel John Lawrence from the party at this point remains a mystery. His Trotskyist past was well known and his closest associate from that time, Gerry Healy, was expelled. The magazine he edited and the associate organisation that he effectively directed had both now been banned. He had been stood down as a parliamentary candidate and his commitment to one of Labour's founding principles, parliamentary democracy, was questionable. Yet Lawrence was allowed to remain as a party member and local councillor. Perhaps the NEC assumed that another expulsion would be more trouble than it was worth and that Lawrence was effectively neutered. If so, the subsequent events in St Pancras showed that they could not have been more wrong.

St Pancras and John Lawrence

Without a weekly magazine to edit, Lawrence was now free to devote far more time and energy to St Pancras Council and local Labour politics. He had been elected as a Labour councillor in the spring of 1953 and in 1955 – less than a year after the ban on *Socialist Outlook* – he was also elected as Chairman of the

Holborn and St Pancras South party. He was re-elected in 1956. For the next five years John Lawrence dominated the politics of St Pancras, and it therefore is impossible to understand the why the riots happened in St Pancras without understanding his pivotal role. There are three main reasons for this.

First, Lawrence's leftist views ran with the grain of the local politics. The local party was a typically Bevanite and the party consistently voted for a Bevanite ticket at the annual elections to the NEC. The CLP could also be relied upon to take a radical position on most local and national issues. Locally, for example, in 1952 the Party opposed the erection of a statue to the late George VI in the area and argued that the money would be better spent on cancer research. Nationally, they offered frequent advice to the NEC about Party policy. In 1953 they demanded that the next Labour government nationalise land and all major industries and later called on the NEC to organise a 'massive campaign of demonstrations and petitions to get the Tory Government to resign'.

The local party's fondness for debating radical resolutions rather than administer the affairs of the party did not go down well at the regional or national level. In 1951 the London agent, James Cattermole, turned up to give the Holborn and St Pancras Labour Party General Management Committee (GMC) a dressing down. Without wasting words, Cattermole told the GMC that policy was only important at election times and 'that this Party spends too much time passing resolutions' when what it should aim for is 'a long inert membership who paid fees, took no interest in politics, did not attend ward meetings and passed no resolutions'. No doubt central office bureaucrats from across the political spectrum have itched to share reflections like this with local activists over the years but they did not go down well in Holborn and St Pancras. The GMC passed yet another resolution, condemning Cattermole's remarks.

The CLP also had extensive contact with both the Socialist Fellowship, *Socialist Outlook* and an extensive overlap with the

Bevanite tide. These links involved both the Party and the MP. Local CLP members had been involved with the journal from the outset and local MP Santo Jeger (*see* chapter 9) had been an occasional contributor, but the connection was also institutional. After the general election defeat in 1950, Socialist Fellowship called a conference at the Holborn Hall to discuss 'Labour and the Future'. The Holborn and St Pancras South Labour Party sent a delegate and the meeting, which was addressed by Brockway, Lawrence and Santo Jeger. When Santo Jeger died suddenly in the autumn of 1953, *Socialist Outlook* called on activists to help his widow and Labour candidate Lena Jeger at the by-election (*see* chapter 9). After the election was over, the CLP secretary thanked *Socialist Outlook* readers, some of whom 'had travelled long distances', for their help in the campaign. *Socialist Outlook* thought the result itself vindicated calls for a more aggressive approach to the Tories. Underneath a front-page picture of Jeger being carried aloft from the town hall it commented: 'How much greater would the enthusiasm be throughout the country if the leaders of the party were to initiate a real campaign to get the Tories out.'

Secondly, Lawrence had gathered a small group of close supporters such as Hilda Lane and David Goldhill, who began to take over important positions with the local party. These people were also, apparently, part of the entrist clique and although few in number they began to work tirelessly within Holborn and St Pancras. Following the deselection of sitting councillors both Goldhill and Lane joined John Lawrence on St Pancras council in the mid-1950s. Hilda Lane (1891–1961) had been a full-time organiser for the radical Independent Labour Party in the west of England before moving into Trotskyist poltics in the 1930s. At some point during the decade she came into contact with Lawrence and the two of them were firm allies thereafter. While she shared Lawrence's politics, however, she lacked his personal touch – even a sympathetic account of her life described her as an 'austere, unbending and humourless Trotskyist'.

Finally, Lawrence's charismatic personality was equally important and anecdotal evidence of his charm is plentiful. The author of this book found him a beguiling interviewee who had the knack of making anything he said sound as though he were merely stating the obvious with which no rational person could disagree. It was, apparently, a charm he had exercised throughout his life. One newspaper related the story of a meeting where Lawrence addressed a crowd of miners who were intially hostile but so swayed by his oratory that they left the hall with beliefs as red as those of the speaker. When he became the Leader of St Pancras Council in 1956 these gifts came to the fore. The local St Pancras newspaper, not one of his natural supporters, described him as 'a born leader and an idealist with a charm and sincerity which have caused revolutions in lesser countries than our own'. Even a correspondent from the otherwise hostile *Times* newspaper reported that 'Mr John Lawrence has a personal charm not always obvious from his actions and reports of his speeches.' Fellow councillor Peggy Duff remembered Lawrence with affection as a 'curious but likeable man'. She went on to describe how 'his excesses had a charm of their own, a sort of slaphappy up and punch 'em which enlivened the council chamber and even delighted the Tories. When he got up to speak, they would settle down in their seats and enjoy the show.'

Never Having It So Good

Now doubt that one of the reasons why the Tories 'enjoyed the show' of Lawrence's oratory was because splits in the Labour Party left Conservative governments in power for more than a decade, and Lawrence contributed in no small measure to the feuding. The 1950s were not propitious years for a socialism – revolutionary or otherwise. Whatever the critics said, the Attlee government had pushed through a major transformation in British society. The welfare state, the NHS and redistribution of wealth were cornerstones of a new settlement which lasted until the arrival of Margaret Thatcher thirty years later.

Macro-economic policy was dubbed 'Butskelism', conjoining the name of the Tory Chancellor of the Exchequer, Butler, with his opposite number, Labour's Hugh Gaitskell.

The image of the decade as one of political consensus and economic prosperity was summed up in the summer of 1957 when Prime Minister Harold Macmillan told a Tory rally in Bedford that 'most of our people have never had it so good'. Macmillan's boast that life was getting materially better for many in the post-war era was a truism not just for Britain but throughout the Western world. The US economy was booming and continental Europe was recovering fast from the war: the Germans began to enjoy the fruits of *'wirtschaftswunder'*, their economic miracle, while the French set off on three decades of extraordinary economic growth known as the *'trente glorieuses'*. On this full tide of global prosperity the British boat rose, too. National output (GDP) increased at an average annual rate of 2.7 per cent between 1950 and 1960. This was enough to ensure that wages grew strongly and in real terms (i.e. after inflation) the average weekly wage – some £16 – was worth around twice as much in 1963 as it had been in 1947. There was more cheering news for workers because just about everyone looking for a job could find one – the average rate of unemployment throughout the 1950s and 1960s hovered around 2 per cent. Inflation also remained low and industrial relations were generally good with the number of days lost to strikes at around 3 million a year. (It was not until the 1970s that the post-war settlement broke down: the annual average of days lost to strikes shot up to over 12 million during that decade and peaked at 30 million days lost in 1979.)

With increasing affluence came increasing consumption and the corresponding boom in consumer durables was one of the most prominent features of the 1950s. Newspapers of the period are stacked with advertisements about the latest labour-saving devices or luxuries for the modern home. One Labour councillor in St Pancras, Barry Bucknell, was a very visible face of the consumer age (*see* chapter 9). Bucknell was a television handyman who presented a show for the BBC on home improvement which had an ever larger following as television grew more popular. In 1952 some 20 million British people huddled around 3 million television sets to watch the coronation of Elizabeth II, but ten years later nearly 12.5 million TV licences were issued and commercial television stations joined 'auntie' in broadcasting to the nation.

Yet not everyone could afford these new gadgets and the rise in living standards was evolutionary rather than revolutionary. In 1951 nearly four out of ten homes had neither a bath nor a shower and even by the early 1960s more than one in five homes had no hot water tap. Central heating, of course, was to be found only in the wealthiest homes – but that was less than 10 per cent of all houses. In 1956 fewer than one in ten British households had a refrigerator; less than one in four homes were 'on the phone' and almost half the homes in Britain were without a washing machine. Car ownership grew steadily but was still for the few, not the many: some 7 per cent of the population owned a car in 1949, a figure that did not reach 50 per cent until 1964. But statistics also reveal how the 'affluent society' disguised an uneven distribution of wealth. By 1964, more than three-quarters of people described as professional or managerial had a car, while less than a third of semi-skilled manual workers managed to keep up with the national average.

Despite the promising macro-economic data, there was also a profound sense of unease expressed with increasing anxiety as the 1950s wore on and rolled into the 1960s. Britain was doing well but others were doing even better and there was something not quite right with the country. Countless articles and books such as Michael Shanks *Stagnant Society* or Anthony Sampson's *Anatomy of Britain* attempted to get to the root of the problem and they identified various causes for concern. Although Britain was doing well by historical standards, it was falling behind its competitors. Growth was good but it was less than half that being recorded by international competition such as West Germany

(7.9 per cent) or Japan (7.7 per cent). And the British share of world trade in manufactured products fell from 25 per cent in 1950 to just 14 per cent in 1964. As other countries became more productive and competitive, there was a dearth of investment in British industry and so it lagged behind, making do with anything that came to hand. The *Daily Telegraph* industrial correspondent Nicholas Comfort described how in 1961 around half of British metal-using industries were using pre-1948 machinery and sometimes it was a lot older: in the 1950s, for example, a giant rolling mill engine was installed in Sheffield's River Don works to shape nuclear reactor shields. The machine had originally been built in 1905 to make armour plate for the Dreadnought battleships.

There was a feeling that Britain was living on past glories and failing to keep up with the times or modernise its industry. If Labour relations seemed to be good it was at least in part because of restrictive practises backed up by the threat of industrial action. Trade union membership rose from 9.5 million members in 1950 to nearly 10 million in 1960 (the increase went on until the 1980s, when union membership went into a sharp decline). In 1964 around half those in the British labour force were still manual workers and the plethora of individual unions frequently resisted the introduction of more efficient and technologically up to date machinery.

On the other side, capital – the owners, managers and shareholders of firms – seemed equally incapable of change. The lack of research and development, shoddy product design, outdated management techniques or elementary understanding of customers was summed up by one executive of the ailing Norton motorbike manufacturer, who insisted that 'most motorcyclists love to spend their Sunday mornings taking off the cylinder head and reseating the valves'. Really? The industrial zeitgeist was brilliantly captured in the Boulting brothers' classic film *I'm Alright Jack* (1959), in which the posh, incompetent young graduate Stanley Windrush (played by Ian Carmichael) lands a job at his uncle's factory. Strikes and uproar follow Windrush's attempts to establish his authority on the shop-floor which is controlled by the communist union convener Fred Kite (played by Peter Sellers) and social divisions are laid bare. In 1941 George Orwell famously described Britain as 'the most class-ridden country under the sun', and twenty years later it seemed to many as though little had changed.

While the Conservatives dominated British national politics in the 1950s, they were very much on the defensive in London because the metropolis remained stubbornly left wing. Labour took control of the London County Council (LCC) – the regional coordinating authority for the inner London boroughs – in the 1930s and held it for the next three decades. For most of that time the LCC was firmly led by Sir Isaac 'Ike' Hayward, who had started work in the mines of his native Wales aged twelve and, like many, had come to the city for work. The Hayward gallery on the South Bank arts complex bears his name. LCC elections were held every three years and Labour's majorities were normally robust with the exception of 1949 when the poll returned sixty-four labour councillors, sixty-four Conservatives and one Liberal. It was said to be the only period that anyone paid any real attention to the Liberal councillor during his entire political career.

Support for Labour in the capital grew steadily again during the 1950s and spiked in 1958 when the party won 101 seats reducing the Tories to their lowest level ever – just twenty-five seats. Yet the division between London and other parts of the country were patent when, a year later, the Tories won a landslide victory at the general election of 1959 and increased their majority in Westminster. Tory irritation with Labour's domination of London grew in the early 1960s and the LCC was merged in 1965 as part of the larger GLC. This took in suburban, Tory-voting, outer London boroughs which made the capital easier to control until the 1980s. When that too inconvenienced the Conservative government, Margaret Thatcher simply abolished the GLC in 1986.

St Pancras was a typical central London borough which was normally held by Labour in the post-war era although, according to Peggy Duff, it mattered little which party controlled the town hall. Elected in 1953, Duff described the period as 'abysmally dull' and explained that:

> Since the end of the war the council had swung with each election, first Labour, then Tory, then Labour again … there was not all that much difference between them. Certainly there was much more cooperation between the very orthodox Labour leader, Fred Powe, and the Tories than between Fred and his backbenches. Council meetings were brief. Occasionally we were treated to a measured speech, usually on libraries, and, once a year, on the rates. Backbenchers slept on the backbenches.

But all that was about to change. In 1956 the local elections returned another Labour majority in St Pancras but immediately after the election there was a minor coup in the Labour group. The ultra-orthodox Fred Powe was ditched and replaced by the charismatic John Lawrence. The next few years would be anything but dull and St Pancras was about to become one of the most talked about councils in the country.

Chapter 3

THE PEOPLES' REPUBLIC OF
ST PANCRAS

British Movietonews are justly proud of the pictures they secured of the May Day trouble outside St Pancras Town Hall. Not only do they show the Red Flag being hoisted but also close-ups, with sound, of rival speakers, police intervention and the final arrests. Dramatically exclusive pictures, they will have aroused as much interest as those of the FA Cup Final in the same issue.

Daily Cinema, 7 May 1958

St Pancras is a Metropolitan Council and not, as hasty readers might suppose, a Soviet Republic ... There are a good number of Boroughs under the control of the Labour Party but none where the communist influence has been so obvious.

Western Morning News, March 1958

In May 1958 there were local elections across the country and the campaign was in full swing. Television was of growing importance and one of the talking points of the campaign was the Conservative Party political broadcast. It opened not, as one might have expected, with shots of Tory politicians boasting of their municipal record or kissing babies, but instead with the image of a red flag flying proudly over St Pancras town hall while the Tories' local government supremo, Geoffrey Rippon MP, warned voters menacingly that 'this is only a symbol but it is an ominous one'. The Tories did not have to mock up the image. A red flag really had been flown from the roof of St Pancras town hall just a few days before, triggering a national howl of outrage, a media firestorm and street brawling during which several councillors were arrested. It was just one of a series of high-profile policies adopted by St Pancras council which attracted nationwide attention – and then led to mass expulsions from the Labour group.

Few would have guessed any of these events were in the offing when Labour again won a majority of seats on St Pancras Council in May 1956. Labour did well across the whole of London; despite its drubbing at the general election just a few months before, the party remained popular in in the capital winning control of twenty councils to the Tories' eight. St Pancras became something of a dividing line. To the north, south and west it was bordered by four of the Conservative councils: Hampstead, Holborn, St Marylebone and Westminster City. Yet on the eastern boundary was Islington, where Labour held every seat.

As the new council was convened for the first time in May 1956, members settled back into their plush seats in the hemicycle of the council chamber. The inaugural session was mainly intended to deal with the formalities of electing the new office holders and expected to be short. As Labour had held the council these would, of course, be the same as the previous incumbents. A long standing pillar of London Labour politics, Fred Powe was to be confirmed as the leader. Evelyn Dennington, a worthy who later became Lady Dennington, would continue as chief whip.

Then, almost out of nowhere, trouble began. A row developed over the arcane issue of the allocation of aldermanic seats. Aldermen were members who were not elected but appointed to join the council (an ancient, undemocratic tradition which has now disappeared). It transpired that a somewhat complicated agreement had been made in 1953 between the Party leaders about the distribution of the aldermanic seats on the council –

each party would nominate one alderman for every six council seats it held. There were ten aldermen in all who were appointed to sit for six years each. Five of them stood down at the election of May 1956 and the other five would retire in 1959. Most of those standing down were Tories and, according to the agreement, they should have been replaced by Tories. While Powe was happy to honour the agreement he had made, he had not bothered to tell others in the Labour group. They felt that they had been kept in the dark and were disgruntled. One moved that Labour break Powe's agreement and take all the seats. Councillor Peggy Duff described what happened next: 'Fred made a very unwise move. "If you pass this resolution," said he, "I will resign as leader." They passed it. He resigned. So did the newly elected chief whip. There was a horrible silence. Then someone nominated John Lawrence (to take over as leader). There were no further nominations. Fred was out and John was in.' Duff then remarked, with studied understatement, 'St Pancras was also in for five years of turbulence.'

The Conservatives were predictably furious that Labour had reneged on the deal and called for the annual mayor-making, normally a pleasant ceremonial occasion with polite chat, tea and sandwiches, to be adjourned. Timothy Donovan, leader of the Tory group, claimed that agreements to share out the aldermanic seats were common practice on many councils, including the LCC. Lawrence replied airily that the agreement had been made over the heads of the people of St Pancras who had just re-elected a majority of Labour candidates; the Conservatives, he said, with the uncompromising insouciance that was his political trademark, 'would have to make the best of it.' These brusque exchanges were entirely out of character with the normal run of things in St Pancras and the local newspaper gossip columnist was perplexed:

What has happened I do not know, but, the overthrowing of an agreement in a belligerent and extremely unpleasant manner and the leader of the council telling the other side to make the best of it was redolent of a totalitarian mind. I would hesitate to come to conclusions but I have suspicions that some of the new, or comparatively new, recruits to Labour in St Pancras may be dyed a deeper 'red' than the rest of their colleagues.

These turned out to be more prescient words than the writer could possibly have guessed.

'The Most Famous Mayor in the Country'

The seizing of the aldermanic seats was soon followed up by another attack on civic pomp. In the spring of 1957 councillors voted to slash the annual mayoral allowance from £1,795 to just £300. The move was designed to save the council money and send out a political message. Council leader Lawrence asserted that the mayoralty had a purely social function which was 'absolutely useless ... This sort of civic tradition and ceremony has nothing to do with working class people.' The local press was scathing. 'What is the point of having a Mayor without pomp and tradition?' it questioned before thundering on about a figurehead who embodied 'civic pride and local independence ... the holder of an office which has existed for centuries and which has lent colour and pageantry to public life'. Several members of the Labour group agreed. Unlike Lawrence, they thought the mayor enjoyed considerable working-class support. When it came to the vote, they defied a three-line whip and abstained – a decision for which they were privately 'hauled over the coals' in the words of one. The argument in the Labour group, however, was as nothing compared to the debate the decision triggered around the country.

As so often in St Pancras, what began as a local row soon spilled national news story: the mayor of St Pancras suddenly became a talking point throughout the country. Up and down the land, local media examined the functions, terms and conditions of their local mayors and Fleet Street leader writers had fun with the story too. When it emerged that the penniless mayor had held an official reception for seventy American visitors from Camden, New Jersey but had no funds to pay – each guest had been asked to chip in 2*s* 6*d* – the *Daily Sketch* offered to foot the bill in a cheeky editorial headlined 'His Worship Mr-can't-afford-it'. 'I couldn't afford to give them a free tea out of the Mayor's allowance. I'm not a millionaire – and 70 teas cost quite a bit of money,' complained the real mayor.

During the original debate, in a question which was to reverberate around the country, Lawrence had asked 'what is wrong with making the mayor go to a school children's party on a 68 bus? In fact, he will be the most famous mayor in the country.' The last part was certainly true and in another editorial, *The Times* leader writer took up the challenge of answering Lawrence's question

> So crammed and overflowing with fascination that it cannot be ignored ... All hinges of course on what the Mayor is to wear ... A Mayor in mufti, a Mayor incognito can travel on a 68 or any other bus he likes and not an eyebrow will be raised ... (but) the children – and this is surely the point which the councillor has overlooked – would expect the Mayor to look like someone who has mistaken the function for a fancy dress ball and would be grievously disappointed if he did not ...

At least one of Labour's leaders agreed. Before the war, Labour's deputy leader, Herbert Morrison, had been mayor of Hackney and had initially followed an instruction from the organisation of London Labour mayors forbidding the wearing of robes and regalia because they were held to be an insult to the unemployed. But when Morrison went to a children's Christmas party in his usual brown suit and red tie the reception was muted. Morrison recalled that 'their faces fell with disappointment and disillusion when I walked in … When I saw this childish reaction I said to myself "we've made a mistake". The office matters more than the man; the children think we've let the position of mayor down.'

For all the frippery surrounding the decision, the suspension of the mayoral allowance had a serious side and signalled a new direction for St Pancras council. Most Labour councillors wanted to control their local authorities in order to use the machinery of the council to improve the lives of their citizens. Very few, if any, wanted the control in order to effectively dismantle institutions like the mayoralty or dominate the aldermanic seats. John Lawrence undoubtedly wanted to improve local services but he also wanted to shape the council to fit the image of what he thought a local council should look like. In the spirit of the revolutionary that he was, he wanted to start from zero.

The decision was also symbolic of an almost puritanical commitment, more in the tradition of non-conformist Roundheads. Harold Wilson once said that the British Labour Party owes more to Methodists than to Marx. Certainly many of the St Pancras councillors felt that they should look, walk and talk like the working people they represented and the mayoral allowance was not the only one they sought to forego. The St Pancras Labour group also opposed the idea councillors should claim for travel expenses to meetings or even postage costs incurred on council business. This was a long time before parliamentary expenses had been introduced and when even MPs had to pay for their own postage when replying to constituent's letters. For privately wealthy Tories, such a regime was not troublesome, but many Labour MPs found the extra expenses far more onerous. Exactly what level of remuneration and expenses should be paid to public representatives is an argument which comes around like the daffodils in spring but perhaps the final, most conclusive comment came from the 'guinea pig' of the experiment, Councillor Redman. Mayor Redman was initially an enthusiastic supporter of the cut in the allowance but his experience of the high office left him battered and exhausted. He missed the official handover to the new mayor, Tom Barker, in March 1958 because he had to wait for a bus. When he did finally turn up to the ceremony, half an hour late and a little breathless, he told his guests that he had regretted that he had not been able to attend more functions but 'it is impossible for the Mayor to carry out his duties properly without official transport.'

Political Histrionics and Histrionic Politics

St Pancras council had more success in bringing colour to London life when it supported the arts. The district had long been a favourite of artists and writers. Whole coteries of artists had found a home in the area, from the pre-Raphaelite Brotherhood to others which also took their names from it such as the Bloomsbury Group, the Euston Road Group or the Camden Town Group. Other great writers such as Dorothy L. Sayers, Mary Shelley, Charles Dickens, J. M. Barrie, Robert Louis Stevenson or Graham Greene made their home in the area and George Bernard Shaw had even been a member of the St Pancras vestry (predecessor of the council).

In the 1950s St Pancras council organised an annual arts festival which helped to cheer up a generally dreary London. The festival was commended by the *New Statesman* as an example of how a local authority could escape from the 'drains and street lighting' image and use some of the rate revenue to broaden and brighten up the lives of the local people. Tony Crossland, one of the Labour Party's younger and more flamboyant leaders, argued that this was exactly the kind of thing which Labour councils should be doing. In his seminal book *The Future of Socialism*, Crosland argued that Labour needed to get away from the old class-based politics, embrace aspiration and be the party of fun. In one passage he argued that:

> We need not only higher exports and old age pensions but more open air cafes, brighter and gayer streets at night, later closing hours for public houses, more local repertory theatres ... brighter and cleaner eating houses ... more murals and pictures in public places, better designs for furniture ... statues in the centre of new housing-estates, better designed street-lamps and telephone kiosks, and so on ad infinitum.

Apart from broadening the festival, the council soon became involved in a more overtly political show. In May 1957, in an act of international solidarity, the council sponsored a concert for the black American civil rights campaigner, Paul Robeson, at the town hall. Robeson was a well-known figure in both the world of music and politics before and after Second World. He was one of the first black graduates from Colombia Law School and a football player talented enough to have become a professional but it was with his music that Robeson commanded an international audience – his gravelly bass voice has an unmistakable quality and was a favourite with audiences in the worlds of opera and jazz. Robeson used his fame to promote two causes which brought him into conflict with the US authorities: communism and civil rights. Forbidden to leave the USA because of his 'un-American activities' Robeson became an international cause célèbre on the left. The highlight of the concert was a performance by Robeson himself, who chatted and sang over the phone for fifteen minutes from his home in New York. It was soon followed up by an even more important event directly connected with minorities in London. The Notting Hill carnival is now the largest Caribbean festival in Europe and it has its origins in St Pancras, where the council began to sponsor a Caribbean festival in the late 1950s. The borough's

Caribbean-born population was relatively small, however, and the carnival was subsequently moved to Notting Hill, which had a far bigger West Indian population.

The council's involvement with the arts became much more controversial in the summer of 1957. The left-wing Unity theatre, housed in a disused chapel at the back of St Pancras station, was a local arts theatre with a national profile; household names of the British stage like Lionel Bart, Alfie Bass, Warren Mitchell, Michael Gambon, Bob Hoskins and Bill Owen learned their stagecraft there. The Unity had been founded in 1936 by an amalgam of trade unions as a focal point of resistance to the rising menace of fascism – early performances mocked Oswald Mosley's British Union of Fascists while others supported Republican forces in the Spanish Civil War. But by the late 1950s, it was struggling to survive.

Television – the social media of the 1950s – became increasingly popular, leaving live theatre performing in front of half-empty houses on ever tighter budgets. During this decade several of London's theatres were in trouble. Many of the older, smaller theatres and music halls had been lost in the Blitz and never replaced. The iconic Holborn Empire for example, where Marie Lloyd had titillated audiences and local lad Dan Leno left them rocking in the aisles, had been boarded up since receiving a direct hit during the Blitz. It was demolished in 1960 and replaced by offices of the Prudential Insurance Company (*see* chapter 5). Public alarm at the loss of venues for live entertainment became increasingly vocal as the 1950s wore on and were even fought out in Parliament. St Pancras North MP Kenneth Robinson became involved high-profile campaigns to save Her Majesty's Theatre in the Haymarket and the St James' Theatre in Covent Garden (which was lost).

Other smaller local venues disappeared too. In 1957, *The Scotsman* newspaper lamented, 'London has already lost many small neighbourhood and experimental theatres such as the Torch, the Old Watergate and the Boltons'. A name very nearly added to that list was that of the Unity in St Pancras. The Unity was very much a grass-roots community centre where productions pioneered new techniques to highlight social issues. In an era when all play scripts had to be approved by the censorious Lord Chamberlain – a practice only wound up in 1968 – the Unity's improvised performances led to clashes with the authorities. The theatre was also a centre for agitation and propaganda ('agitprop') and if there was a common theme to productions it was working class struggle; naturally it had strong links to the Left Book Club and the Communist Party.

The manager of the Unity, with the appropriately stagey name of Heinz Bernard, complained that 'a large proportion of their once regular audience now apparently preferred to stay at home and twiddle knobs on their television sets'. Even cinema was suffering – audiences were falling and some 70 per cent of films shown in British cinema came from the USA – and against these social trends and the chances of the Unity attracting back a large, regular local audience were slim. A further problem stemmed from the somewhat restricted appeal of the plays staged at the Unity. Few of the productions were crowd pullers. The long list of pantomimes and revues produced there were concerned with social struggles and with titles such as *Waiting for Lefty*, a cradle of popular culture it was not. The show running in August 1957, for example, called *Cyanide*, was described in one review a 'vigorous, moving story set in a small industrial community in the US'. Little wonder that the audiences preferred television at home. The limited scope of the theatre was well illustrated by another review a month later:

> The present production of *The Matchgirls* ... shows the struggle of the factory girls of 1888 for better conditions of work – not in itself an enticing theme for an evening's entertainment in the theatre. The producer has attempted to enliven the proceedings in the fashionable style of the late Bertholt Brecht. The lyrics

are blasphemous and semi-obscene, and certainly make one sit up ... As a piece of historic reconstruction the play is reasonably interesting and it is a pleasant change to see unskilled workers sympathetically presented on the London stage ... But *The Matchgirls* is too full of class hatred to have any relevance for the present day.

By summer 1957 the theatre was wobbling on the verge of bankruptcy. An appeal for £3,000 was launched by a group of friends, which included artists Lewis Casson, Sybil Thorndike, Wolf Mankowitz and MP Bessie Braddock. Then St Pancras decided to take a leading role in the appeal and in July the council agreed to grant the Unity £300. The council argued that the Unity was a community asset that deserved support. Although some of the productions could best be described as esoteric, the theatre did have deep roots in the local community and ordinary (non-professional) people were encouraged to become involved in every aspect of the Unity's productions; the LCC ran drama classes in the theatre and local OAPs were among those who could get in free. The council were easily persuaded that it was a worthy cause.

Local opinion about the grant was divided, however. The local press, which described the Unity as 'a dismal theatre supported by hair-suit intellectuals', condemned it while conceding that it did contain a peculiar logic if only because 'histrionic politics have come to the rescue of political histrionics'. In the tradition of all those who ever oppose subsidies to the arts (except, perhaps, opera), the paper argued that if the people of St Pancras really wanted to see the type of plays produced there they would pay at the box office to go and see them but should not be forced to do so through the rates. Other reactions were more sympathetic. One national magazine applauded the council and argued that 'this is a fine example to other local authorities who are often reluctant to support living theatre ... The actors and staff are nearly all amateurs which makes one eager to praise their enthusiasm in these days when few people can be bothered to provide their own entertainment.'

In the event, the debate was cut short by the Conservative minister responsible for local government, Henry Brooke, who simply vetoed the grant. The council were trying to make the money over to the Unity under section 136 of the Local Government Act 1948 which needed ministerial approval – something that Brooke refused to do. He also refused to say exactly why he was blocking the application: when a journalist from *The Times* tried to find out what was going on he was told that 'it is a matter for St Pancras to take up with us directly; even then it does not follow we shall give a reason'. These were still the days when freedom of information remained a distant concept.

By November 1957 the Unity was desperate for money. With a suitably dramatic turn of phrase the manager Heinz Bernard commented that 'this is practically a matter of life and death for us. The money was needed to pay the rates of £250.' He added with a touch of malevolence 'our next production is a Christmas show – you can be sure Mr Brooke will figure in it' and for good measure he sent the minister two complimentary tickets. The row simmered on and on, however, generating reams of comment in the media until, at the eleventh hour, the council hit on a new idea to fund the Unity. By using a different section of local government legislation, it could subsidise individual productions rather than the theatre as such and this did not require ministerial approval. Another wave of press comment followed and the *Daily Mail* – predictably – was furious. After a half-line nod to democratic pluralism the paper launched an extraordinary editorial attack on the small theatre and the £300 grant was presented as a threat to democracy itself.

Though tolerance is a virtue which is highly prized by most Britons, it is patently foolish to stretch it to the extent of actually assisting those who intend to do us harm. Yet ... St Pancras Borough Council ... blandly proposes to hand over £300 of the ratepayers' money as a gift to the Unity Theatre. And the Unity Theatre exists for the openly-avowed purpose of presenting nothing but left-wing plays ... If it is argued that a democratic system must permit full expression even to dangerous creeds, the answer surely is that democracy thus risks signing its own death warrant. To put it bluntly need we be tender to those who eagerly seek to destroy us?

Deciding where the limits of freedom of expression lie, and especially artistic freedom, has stimulated arguments in Britain for centuries. It continues to this day. But for the *Daily Mail* – which just twenty years before ran a notorious editorial praising Oswald Mosley's fascists headlined 'Hurrah for the Blackshirts' – to raise questions about 'those who would destroy us' was beyond even Shakespearean irony.

The wider impression, however, was of St Pancras council once again at the centre of a national controversy. Behind the bluster, on both sides, there was a more serious point to be made. The Unity was in part responsible for its own difficulties because of its narrow, sectarian artistic policy and it never really sought to escape from its doctrinal base. Yet a new cultural challenge to established order did emerge in the mid-1950s, and it was one which superseded any threat posed by the Unity: Angry Young Men were popping up everywhere to rail against traditional values. Books like Colin Wilson's *The Outsider* and plays like John Osborne's play *Look Back in Anger* both appeared for the first time in 1956. They unleashed a fresh energy for a new a new direction in British art even if the destination remained unclear.

Audiences were shocked – some even walked out of the premier at the Royal Court theatre in Sloan Square – when Jimmy Porter, the central character of *Look Back in Anger* launched vicious diatribes against his innocent wife Alison. Colin Wilson was just twenty-four when he published his first book, *The Outsider*, and declared himself to be 'the major literary genius of our century'. Wilson slept rough in a sleeping bag on Hampstead Heath and bused it down through St Pancras to the reading room of the British Museum library in Holborn where he wrote the book. It was a huge success – at least among the *bien pensant* literary critics who turned Wilson into a cult figure. Drawing from, among others, on Friedrich Nietzsche, Jean-Paul Sartre, Albert Camus, Ernest Hemingway, Vaslav Nijinsky, Vincent van Gogh, Hermann Hesse and Lawrence of Arabia, the young Wilson offered up a garbled version of existentialism. He was lionised in gushing reviews even by some (like Cyril Connolly) who later confessed that they had never actually read the book and it was a literary equivalent of the *Mary Celeste* – massive interest generated by a vessel without content. John Lawrence was contemptous from the start. In an interview with the *Sunday Times* he explained his view that the ordinary working classes were the most cultured, intelligent and progressive people in Britain. 'What literature have the middle classes produced?' he asked. 'Only the personal sweatings of well-fed intellectuals, the wafflings of Osborne.'

The Most Freakish Borough in London

Lawrence's comments about John Osborne in the *Sunday Times* appeared just five days before another gesture which attracted nationwide notoriety and debate – the raising of a red flag on the Town Hall roof on 1 May 1958. While an angry young playwright was upending cultural norms in Chelsea, the red flag affair in St Pancras was, according to Councillor Peggy Duff 'a rather old fashioned campaign'. In most of continental Europe the celebration of May Day with red flags, banners and a holiday by parties of the left passed without comment but the day had never caught on in Britain. 'So when St Pancras decided to give all staff a holiday on that day and, in addition, to fly the Red Flag from the Town Hall, the emotional impact, especially on the Tories, was instantaneous and large. You would have thought that a communist take-over of the borough was imminent,' recalled Duff. The consequence was that, around the country and for years after, St Pancras was tagged as the 'Red Flag borough'.

The idea to fly a red flag from the roof of the town hall on May Day came from the septuagenarian Father of the Council, Tom Barker. After an extraordinary life (*see* chapter 9), Barker was an old living quietly in St Pancras and had one last firework to produce. At the General Purposes committee meeting in late February 1958 Barker made the apparently innocuous suggestion that a red flag be flown from the town hall on May Day and that the council's 1,300 employees be given the day off to celebrate the occasion. Barker, of course, was exactly the sort of socialist for whom the red flag symbolised the solidarity of the international working class which he had spent an eventful life trying to promote. It did not take the press long to sniff another juicy story coming from St Pancras. The *Daily Telegraph* was first on the trail when it commented disdainfully that 'clearly the local socialists are anxious for another dose of cheap notoriety'. The story gathered momentum when it was picked up by the provincial press, which also began to look more closely at John Lawrence. One ran a feature on his Trotskyist past and warned that 'people who live in St Pancras should take a careful look at their local council. Under the leadership of the cloth-capped Mr John Lawrence it is planning to fly the Red Flag ... the latest in a number of strange actions.' The *London Evening News* was also concerned and devoted an entire editorial to St Pancras, which concluded, 'It is not surprising ... that St Pancras is rapidly establishing itself as London's most freakish borough council'.

A heated row about the red flag proposal followed at the next council meeting in which the Tories accused Labour of wasting ratepayers' money and using 'the language of class war'. Much of the debate centred on the different interpretations of what it was exactly the flag stood for: internationalism? Workers' rights? The USSR? No one seemed quite sure but it was another comment of John Lawrence's which really ignited the meeting. After describing the Red Flag, as 'the most noble symbol that ever flew in the world', he went on to reflect, 'I look forward to the day when it will be flying not only over the Houses of Parliament but over Buckingham Palace as well.'

At this point supporters of Oswald Mosley's Union Movement in the public gallery erupted and attempted to break up the meeting. Cries of 'filthy reds', 'dirty traitors' and 'we've got to get rid of the Yids' rang out across the council chamber as the fascists hurled bundles of leaflets headed 'No Red Flag Here' onto the councillors below. The mayhem continued as the galleries were cleared with Lawrence's supporters singing lusty choruses of the 'Red Flag' anthem as they went. There was general agreement in the extensive press coverage that the fascists had started the trouble, but little sympathy for Labour. The *Daily Star*, for example, harrumphed that 'no wonder there were noisy fascists in the galleries. Hysterical extremists of left and right are brothers under the skin. You can hardly hoist a red flag without trailing a black flag too'. The *London Evening News* also went back on the attack, commenting:

> The antics of the Socialists on St Pancras Borough Council have long since ceased to be a joke ... the flag is the symbol of class war, and the class war is an evil ... which the British people regardless of party have firmly and wisely rejected. To wave this banner of violence and bigotry and intolerance in London is as ugly and malevolent as to give a chance to the Mosleyites to snatch the Union Flag and pretend to patriotism. A plague on them all.

The following day, John Lawrence held a press conference that was almost beyond parody. Lawrence was clerk to the shop stewards at Briggs Bodies, part of the massive Ford motor plant in Dagenham where industrial relations were notoriously poor. The previous year, for example, an AEU shop steward nicknamed the 'Bellringer' after his singular method for calling out the workers had been sacked and the ensuing dispute had still not fully settled. Like a scene from the hit film about the parlous state of British industry, *I'm Alright Jack*, Lawrence talked to the media from the shop stewards' office. Cup of tea in hand, it was the perfect setting for Lawrence to elaborate on his speech in the council chamber the night before. He reaffirmed his belief that the red flag would one day fly over Buckingham Palace and went on to suggest that it would be a good idea if the whole building were to be given over to families on the council's waiting list saying 'I believe there are some 500 rooms in it where we could house a lot of people who are shockingly overcrowded at present. The Queen could live somewhere quietly in the country – she's got other houses hasn't she?'

By now, St Pancras had moved on from being 'the most freakish borough' in London to the most famous council in the country. The provincial press was busy vox-popping their local residents and feeding their views back in what became a familiar media loop. Unfortunately for St Pancras, most of the coverage was hostile and over the next two weeks developed a momentum of its own. Lawrence and other councillors were the target of violent threats – as was the flag that had to be smuggled into the town hall. A Tory councillor explained to the press that 'a number of threats have been made to prevent it being flown and the socialists are not taking any chances'.

In an eleventh hour attempt to prevent the flag appearing, the Conservatives presented a 1,500 signature petition and tabled a motion of censure. But they were not alone. The red-flag gesture split the Labour Party and fifteen councillors who wanted nothing to do with it were absent from the council meeting where it was discussed. The Tories now urged these Labour councillors to turn up and help reverse the decision, prompting the *Evening News* to comment, 'it must be the first time in years that councillors have pleaded with opponents to attend.' The Tory leader described the proposal as a 'silly, provocative, spiteful and partisan act ... not promoted by the Labour group in the borough but by a communist faction within it'.

In fact, the Labour group was more deeply divided than he could have known and was indeed about to fall apart (*see* chapter 6). Despite Tory calls for a full attendance, several Labour councillors were absent yet again from the irritable, fractious meeting. Other groups, however, were out in force. The public galleries were packed and extra police on duty behind steel grilles erected around the town hall to keep the crowds at bay. The motion to fly the flag was carried and the following day – the eve of May Day – the Labour leadership issued a statement which did little to calm the tension.

> Since the first May Day was held in Chicago in 1890, May 1 has become the one day in the year when socialists and trade unionists throughout the world reaffirm their beliefs. In view of the open threats made by fascists to 'tear down the red flag' and create public disorder the Labour group asks socialists in the London area to come to St Pancras council's May Day rally opposite the Town Hall ... to prevent fascist interference with Labour's traditional May Day celebrations.

The Tories described the statement as an 'invitation to a fight', and it was followed by a bullish appeal from the communist *Daily Worker*, which was practically a call to arms:

> The decision of St Pancras Town Council to celebrate May Day has aroused the spiteful anger of Tories, fascists and others who hate any manifestation of working class solidarity ... The Labour Group on the council have appealed to people to defeat them. The working class in London and all who believe in peace and the international solidarity of working people should respond to this appeal.

May Day 1958 began quietly enough. As the sun rose in the sky shedding the first light on what would be a beautiful spring day John Lawrence and seven other councillors climbed out on to the town hall roof to unfurl the flag. But the peace was not to last. A widely advertised open-air meeting had been organised by the St Pancras Trades Council – the forum of local trade unions – in nearby Ossulston Street as part of the May Day celebrations. Half way up the street was a large cobbled square, flanked on one side by a housing estate and on the other by the long red-brick walls of the Victorian potato market. When the Trades Council organisers arrived, however, they were disconcerted to find that members of the fascist Union Movement had also been up early. Having set up their platform at about 7.30 a.m., fascists had stood on it all morning gesticulating noiselessly and had only begun to speak as the Trades Council organisers arrived. It was a deliberate provocation but, undeterred, the socialists set up their platform and large Holborn and St Pancras Trades Council banner where they had planned. The two hostile groups were now within yards of each other and the square was soon a chaotic throng of people, some cheering, some jeering and all arguing violently in a dozen different groups. At that point the police began to intervene and make arrests. John Lawrence was speaking on the Trades Council platform when six policemen came from behind, lifted him bodily from the rostrum and bundled the council leader into a police van.

The arrest of the Lawrence further excited the rival groups and fights began. Things got pretty nasty for a while, as the two groups battled it out – one fascist speaker claimed that he was gashed in the eye by a razor blade, which had been thrown embedded in an orange. The gates of the adjacent potato market then opened and mounted police rode out into the narrow street, helping other officers on foot to separate and then disperse the two factions. More arrests were made and people thrown into two police vans which had backed into the square. The local MP, Lena Jeger, then arrived on the scene to try and negotiate with the police and calm things down. She addressed the crowd briefly, but her attempts were in vain. By this time tempers were high and, amid choruses of the Red Flag, the scuffles and fighting intensified. More arrests followed including that of the deputy mayor, Hilda Lane. Eventually the police brought the situation under control but by this time more trouble had flared up outside the town hall a few hundred yards away. Some 200 students had turned up, parading Union Jacks and chanting 'we've got to get rid of the reds' which provoked more scuffles and more people were arrested.

Towards mid-evening a still sizeable crowd around the town hall watched eagerly as John Lawrence emerged onto the roof of the building. At 8.15 p.m. he dipped the fluttering flag in salute and hauled it down amid cheers and jeers from those gathered on the steps of St Pancras station opposite. The flag had survived the day intact but the reputation of the Labour group in St Pancras was in shreds. A total of nineteen people were arrested during the day – including several councillors – on various charges ranging from obstruction to threatening behaviour. The hearing at Clerkenwell Magistrates Court the following day generated almost as much media interest as the original fracas and the press had a field day as journalists crowded into the public gallery. Alongside them sat the two local MPs, watching glumly as the case unfolded.

The exact sequence of events was hard to piece together – even today some of the evidence reads more like a chaotic script from the *Keystone Cops* rather than an example of crisp law enforcement. Much confused and conflicting evidence given – not least from police witnesses who were accused by the defendant's solicitor of perjuring themselves and whose role was subsequently questioned by both local MPs in the House of Commons. Unusually, the police were granted an adjournment so that they could organise legal representation because of what the magistrate described, without exaggeration, as the 'considerable public interest' in the case.

The hearing then dragged on for the next two weeks, all of which created the impression that the disorder had been even more serious than it actually was but the overall effect, of course, was to prolong the media frenzy. Almost all the defendants were found guilty and for the image of the Labour Party it could not have been worse. The most immediate problem was that it brought the St Pancras councillors into conflict with the police – a PR battle they were always destined to lose. The police may have perjured themselves but that is not the way most people saw the events. A typical view was offered by the *Morning Advertiser* in an editorial which claimed that:

> The tradition of free speech must never be surrendered ... Britain is one of the few countries in the world where no political strings are attached. Let that tradition be broken, let the complete confidence of the Briton in his police force be shaken, and the prospects for law and order become dim. We know of police states where the citizen walks in fear.

This 'complete confidence.' was shaken by some of the scandals involving the Metropolitan Police in the 1960s but this was yet to come. Anthropologist Geoffrey Gorer's research into social attitudes in the mid-1950s found a high level of trust in the police, concluding 'the amount and extent of enthusiastic appreciation of the police is particularly English and a most important component of the contemporary English character. To a great extent, the police represent an ideal model of behaviour and character.' According to this interpretation, the police acted to defend the rights of all and the perception which most people were left with was one of anarchy and disorder.

A more profound political problem was that, just at a time when the full horrors of Stalinism were still being absorbed and the 1956 invasion of Hungary was fresh in Western minds, the St Pancras Labour group allowed itself to become conflated with Soviet communism. The timing could not have been worse and in the context of the late 1950s the only thing the red flag achieved was to alienate many Labour voters and moderate supporters. Even normally sympathetic *Daily Mirror* columnist Cassandra rounded on the party:

> [The red flag] is the Russian standard of a way of life that, by horror piled on horror, by violence heaped on persecution, has reached its present terrible eminence. It is the flag which flew from the turrets of the Red Army tanks when they clanked into Budapest. To flaunt Stalin's standard, Beria's standard and Serov's standard, and to pretend that it is the same flag, bearing the same ideals as Kier Hardie's pennant is impudent, provocative rubbish.

Some on the council argued that the red flag was a symbol of international working-class solidarity but again that was not how it was seen to many people. An example of the confusion was evident when a TV quiz show contestant on the show *Who Knows* referred to the 'communist Red Flag which flew over St Pancras Town Hall.' After a complaint from the St Pancras North Labour Party, an apology was broadcast at the start of the following week's programme when it was confirmed that the flag was the symbol of the labour movement, not Soviet communism. The contestant's blunder, however, merely underlined large number of people were muddled about what the red flag actually represented. At best, the gesture simply became the butt of punchlines: in his Sunday night slot at the London Palladian, comedian Tommy Trinder cracked 'they are having great trouble with the trains down at St Pancras station – no one dares to wave the red flag!' The Labour Party hierarchy were among those who failed to see the funny side of the joke.

The noisy ruckus on 1 May in St Pancras were met with an almost universal stony silence from the rest of the labour movement. The only newspaper which backed the Labour councillors was the official organ of the Communist Party, the *Daily Worker* which opined 'in the capitalist world the growing economic crisis is casting a shadow over every working class home ... In St Pancras the place in Britain where there was a May Day celebration, the police closed down the meeting – an act which should give the whole working class movement grave cause for concern'. Yet hardly any workers did express concern. A handful of Trade Union branches sent messages of support to St Pancras but they were the exception. Where voices were raised, it was to distance Labour from the council.

The Red Flag affair could not have come at a worse time for Labour. It flew in the face of the image that the party's national leaders were trying to project. After the final rapprochement between Bevanism and revisionism at Labour's conference in October 1957, Party leaders worked hard to present an image of unity, moderation and cohesion. The Suez affair (November 1956) had left the Tory party on the ropes and Labour's prospects of winning the next general election were looking much improved. Big gains were being made, especially in London where Labour increased its majority on the London County Council after the local elections in April 1958. But then the tide began to turn against Labour in a number of ways. Most importantly, the Tories began to reflate the economy and engineer a short-term economic boom. There was little Labour could do about this but the party then scored a number of own goals. The most important of these was a bus workers' strike, which was widely interpreted as a direct challenge to the government and seriously damaged Labour's image. The Red Flag and the disturbances in St Pancras, which happened just a week before the strike began, could scarcely have been a more appropriate overture to the dispute and soon after these events, opinion began to swing against Labour. By the summer of 1958 polls indicated that the Tories were back in the game. In that context, the Red Flag in St Pancras was nothing more than an irritating distraction. It had nothing useful to say about the future direction of the Party or to offer in terms of winning elections.

Sex and St Pancras

In many ways Peggy Duff was right: the red flag was an old-fashioned protest, one of the last knockings of class-based politics. Profound social changes were afoot but the savy MP Lena Jeger had more insight about what was happening than John Lawrence. In 1962 she wrote an article in the *Political Quarterly* magazine about family planning which she argued was 'one of the little revolutions which have taken place in the lifetime of some of us who do not feel very old, and which is one of the most telling and exiting measurements of social progress'. Jeger charted the history of the birth control movement as one of protest and argued that 'it was a logical development of the suffragette movement'. She reminded readers that birth control pioneer Dr Marie Stopes, who opened her first clinic in St Pancras in the 1920s, had revolutionised the lives of women. Stopes' bestselling book *Married Love* explained contraception in detail, allowing women to enjoy sex without the fear of falling pregnant. As Jeger put it, 'Dr Stopes' readers ... suddenly found that sex was not, after all, something which you had to let a man do to you to keep him quiet and to make babies.'

This was, surely, a real revolution for half of the population. But it was not understood by John Lawrence or his group, which continued to see politics almost wholly through the prism of class conflict. With a broader view, they might have picked up on the embryonic social changes that would lead to the permissive society but that still needed to be fought for. There were important limitations on the use of contraception, for example; ignorance remained and it was almost exclusively married women who sought help. For single women the possibility of falling pregnant remained a terrifying prospect and just one story from the pages of the local paper in St Pancras illustrated why.

At the end of March 1957, a young couple waited nervously outside Finsbury Park tube station. Twenty-two-year old apprentice draftsman, Gerald, and his twenty-year-old girlfriend Maureen had a problem. Maureen was pregnant. They had arranged to meet a man 'with a long cigarette holder' called Frank who was going to help them solve their problem. Frank, a sixty-six-year-old market trader, didn't know much about women's bodies but he knew a man who did. The three of them went to a tea shop where Gerald gave Frank £30 and left him alone with Maureen. Quite what happened next is not clear, but on 1 April Maureen was admitted to hospital with internal injuries so severe that she died. Frank and a sixty-two-year-old vendor of proprietary medicine called Cyril were later arrested, charged and found guilty of performing an illegal operation to procure a miscarriage.

It would be another decade before young women like Maureen could seek safe, legal abortions. But until then, the practice was part of what Jeger described as 'the limberlost of morality which the ambivalence of British politics likes to consider non-political such as homosexuality and prostitution, marriage and divorce, blasphemy and obscenity'. Jeger was very clear that these issues were political and that the real barrier to change was inertia: 'The fact that Parliament must be responsible for the laws of the land in these matters as in all else, and that Parliament is in practice the express will of the people, is a simple fact which it is easier to overlook than explain.'

Like Jeger, the MP for St Pancras North Kenneth Robinson (*see* chapter 9) was in the vanguard of those pressing for change both to the law and social culture in Britain. In 1961 Robinson introduced a Private Members' Bill to reform the abortion law to protect girls like Maureen. It failed, but when he became Minister of Health in the Wilson government, Robinson ensured that another Private Member's Bill introduced by the young Liberal MP David Steel had enough parliamentary time to become law.

Robinson was also the first Chair of the National Association for Mental Health (now Mind) and a pioneer campaigner on mental illness in an age when the subject was even more taboo than it is now; he was particularly vexed that attempted suicide was a criminal offence and in 1958 introduced a Private

Members' Bill to change the law. This was not just a case of tidying up the statute book. In 1956 over 600 people were prosecuted after trying to kill themselves – nearly 10 per cent of failed suicide attempts. The lucky ones were discharged, fined or put on probation, but thirty-three were actually sent to prison. Robinson's Bill to end this judicial lunacy was resisted by the government but his campaign gathered momentum and eventually attempted suicide was decriminalised in 1961.

The most controversial social issue of the decade, however, was reform of the laws criminalising homosexuality and governing prostitution. One evening after the war a man living in Great Ormond Street, Holborn, left his house looking for sex. Not any kind of sex but 'cottaging' – casual sex with other men in public toilets. By his own admission he had 'a life-long, love-hate relationship with lavatories', with the smell, the ambience, the thrill. He could have turned left towards the public toilets in Guildford Street, but chose the slightly longer walk to Jockeys' Fields by the Lincoln's Inn where he propositioned a man in the urinals. On many evenings other men might have been in the toilet for the same reason. But this was not one of those evenings. The shadowy figure standing at the urinal was not a fellow cottager but a policeman, who promptly made an arrest. The man in question was lucky. His name was Tom Driberg, a Labour MP, journalist and one-time writer of the William Hickey gossip column in the *Daily Express*. Driberg was fantastically well connected with just about everyone in London, from high society to the spooks of MI6; as soon as the police realised this, charges were dropped and Driberg went on his way.

Many others were less fortunate. In the mid-1950s, over 1,000 men languished in prison for homosexual acts which were judged to be criminal. Social attitudes were slowly changing, however, and in 1954 the government established the Wolfenden Committee to look at the law on homosexuality and prostitution. In many ways the committee was a study in eccentricity: John Wolfenden was a former headmaster, and to spare the blushes of the ladies on the committee, homosexuals were initially referred to as 'Huntleys' and prostitutes as 'Palmers' (after the famous biscuit makers, Huntley & Palmer). In 1957, the committee proposed decriminalising homosexual behaviour between consenting adults and Kenneth Robinson MP was again in the thick of the fight to make this a reality. He was an executive member of the Homosexual Law Reform Committee and in 1960 introduced the first parliamentary debate on the Wolfenden Report.

In fact, it would be another decade before the law decriminalising sex between consenting men was passed and the forces resisting change overcome. Some were easily anticipated: the conservative right, religious groups and traditionalists, but other voices against reform were less predictable. Glaswegian Labour MP Jean Mann, for example, complained bitterly in her memoirs *Woman in Parliament* (1962) about the focus on homosexuality and singled out Robinson for sponsoring one of the debates in Parliament. 'Does he really believe,' wrote Mann, 'that the people of St Pancras want to wipe sodomy as a crime off the Statute Book – see policemen walking past males procuring males without the power to even caution – and have homosexuals now free to set up house with one another, next door to young families? Has he ever described the full implications of these proposals to the people of St Pancras North?'

Mann thought that homosexual law reform was really only of concern in the metropolis and part of a North–South divide. 'Apart from London and the south,' she wrote, 'the subject is anathema in most constituencies. They frankly do not understand why parliamentary time should be occupied with it.' She also thought that Robinson and his fellow reformers were in a minority, even on the left. 'It would be interesting to know how many resolutions appear on the Labour Party agenda asking for this reform. My own experience is that, for discussion amongst the rank and file, it would be as welcome as reading aloud from Lady C'. (D. H. Lawrence's novel *Lady Chatterley's Lover*, written in the 1920s, had been banned in Britain as 'obscene'. It was only finally published after a lengthy and famous trial in 1960.)

Nobody knew exactly how many prostitutes there were in London in the post-war era. Estimates in the late 1950s varied wildly, but the best guess was of around 3,000 streetwalkers in central London and their visibility added to the nuisance for residents around railway stations like King's Cross and Euston; Wolfenden commented that 'some of the streets of the streets of London are without parallel in the capital cities of other countries'. The Street Offences Act (1959), based on recommendations in Wolfenden, made it easier to charge prostitutes (police no longer needed to prove that the person accosted had been 'annoyed') and penalties were increased. For a while it worked and prostitutes disappeared from the street, but they did not disappear. Many of the street women simply joined those in the bars, clubs or private rooms plying their trade in areas like St Pancras, and Mann found arriving from her native Scotland a painful experience. She quoted a comment from the *Sunday Times* with approval: 'They used to describe Port Said as the wickedest city in the world. To me, London 1960 does not seem far behind. Vice hits the visitor in the face wherever he goes.' She singled out St Pancras as being a particularly depraved area. Banned from actually waking the streets, women flooded local shops with adverts instead, so that Mann observed:

> Vice is so organised that whether a visitor comes out of Euston (or) King's Cross stations ... the nearest shops carrying advertisements for board and lodgings also carry a special board with bright red, yellow and blue notices to inform him how he can contact Continental Blond Stella (unhurried and co-operative) ... Marcelle an exciting blond, The Teenage Model ... The Lady who gives personal attention but 'no coloureds please', Margie who 'has a branch in Nottingham'.

But by now Mann is bewildered. 'How,' she asks, 'does Margie give personal attention in both London and Nottingham?'

Mann complained that 'organised filth' in St Pancras became even worse in the area around her hotel in Russell Square, Holborn. Stepping out of her taxi from the House of Commons she 'found the pavement blocked right out to the street with men, those nearest taking notes, others waiting their turn, and a great deal of chuckling and laughter among them.' She returned the next morning. 'I went around the area and found the whole practice widespread ... The heaviest traffic is during the conference season when thousands of delegates from all over Britain arrive in London.'

Mann wondered why the police in the capital did so little and 'that such advertisements would not be permitted outside London ... Why don't the London Boroughs take powers and why are the Councillors so unconcerned?' Exploitation of women was, like homosexual law reform, family planning and mental health, a serious issue indeed. But in St Pancras, councillors who should have known better were too busy fighting over red flags to worry about things like that.

Chapter 4

WAR GAMES

'All other issues were dwarfed by comparison.'
    Jennie Lee MP and wife of Aneurin Bevan writing about the
    nuclear disarmament debate in Britain in the summer of 1957.

> Then raise the workers' bomb on high,
> Beneath its cloud we'll gladly die,
> For though it sends us all to hell,
> It kills the ruling class as well.
>
> Anon, 1958

The possibility of the Third World War cast a long shadow over
the politics of the 1950s. Exhilaration at the defeat of Nazism
quickly gave way to fears about Soviet expansionism as former
enemies became allies and former allies, enemies. Large parts
of central Europe were now single party communist state and
it was assumed that Moscow had designs on other countries
too. The Cold War threw up many chilling questions: would
the Soviets move into Germany, Austria or ferment trouble in
some other part of the globe? And under what circumstances
might any of this trigger a nuclear exchange? Meanwhile,
the cornerstone of British foreign policy for two centuries –
Empire – was crumbling in the face of independence movements
and the shift of global power from Britain to the USA. The

period truly was, as the poet W. H. Auden had predicted, an 'age of anxiety'.

St Pancras Council and the local Labour Party became directly involved in the arguments. The council was in the national media spotlight when it twinned itself with a small town in communist East Germany – an unusual move at the height of the Cold War – and abandoned its legal obligation to provide civil defence in the event of a nuclear attack. Holborn and St Pancras also became the birthplace of the Campaign for Nuclear Disarmament (CND), the biggest and most innovative protest movement ever seen in post-war Britain.

Budapest and a Small Town in Germany

Unless a nation is actually at war, foreign policy is not normally a priority for most voters. Their interests focus on the domestic issues that touch on their daily lives such as the adequacy of the health service, standards of education or the availability of housing. The autumn of 1956, however, was different and two events occurred which went beyond normal: the Soviet invasion of Hungary and the Suez crisis. Each provided a 'before' and 'after' – events so starkly brutal in their outcome that they changed perceptions about the world for a generation.

In October 1956, a coalition of groups in Hungary joined forces to oust the Moscow-backed communist government in Budapest. A new administration took shape, dedicated to democracy, and for some days it looked as though the uprising would succeed. Then early in November Soviet tanks rolled over the border and into Budapest. With the international community embroiled in the Suez crisis, Hungary was quickly overwhelmed, the revolution crushed and the iron fist of communist rule re-established.

During the turmoil, thousands of refugees fled the country while they had the chance and some of the Hungarians came to St Pancras. They were known as displaced persons or DPs, and like other refugees throughout history – or today – they arrived to a mixed reception. There were fears that the Hungarians would place an intolerable burden on local services, in particular taking jobs and houses from local people. The manager of the Camden employment exchange (job centre) pleaded with locals to show 'a little sympathy and a great deal of consideration' towards the Hungarians looking for work. When a rumour began circulating in neighbouring Islington that new flats were to be given to Hungarian refugees there was uproar; it became the front-page lead story on the local paper and had to be quickly scotched by the local housing chief.

Every Hungarian refugee carried with them their own, individual, moving story, but there were profound political consequences too. In particular, the uprising of November 1956 was a watershed for the international left. The invasion confirmed social democrats in their established abhorrence of the USSR but the shock went much further and even the Communist Party haemorrhaged thousands of disaffected members. In Holborn and St Pancras, however, John Lawrence kept the faith. His pro-Soviet sympathies were well known: they had, after all, caused a deep rift with his erstwhile Trotskyite comrades (*see* Chapter 2). Lawrence now viewed the Russian use of force to suppress dissent in Budapest as a necessary measure. He and his supporters peddled the Soviet line that intervention was merely a response to 'fascist provocation' and argued that the situation in Hungary 'was not at all clear'. But the majority in the local party saw the Soviet outrage for what it was and after a long, heated debate a general party meeting condemned the Soviet intervention. The decision prompted one local activist, Patrick Hutber (who became a well-known journalist in the *Sunday Telegraph*), to send a triumphant note to Labour Party General Secretary, Morgan Phillips:

> Even small victories should not go unrecorded. I thought you might be glad to know that the (Holborn and St Pancras GMC) passed,

after a furious debate, a resolution condemning in the strongest terms the Russian brutality in Hungary and threw out a resolution talking about Fascist provocation. If even St Pancras feels like this, Khrushchev can't have a friend in the world.

As it turned out, Hutber was wrong. John Lawrence had no intention of withdrawing the hand of friendship from Russian president Khrushchev. Just a year after the suppression in Hungary, in October 1957, St Pancras Council received an extraordinary letter from the Mayor of Gera, a small town in communist East Germany. The note suggested that the two authorities twin themselves in an association of friendship and St Pancras agreed to take Gera up on the offer. Once again, St Pancras became the focus of bemused national media comment at this unique town-twinning arrangement. But the puzzlement soon turned to open hostility when the council voted to support a 'peace manifesto' sent from Gera to mark the anniversary of the 1917 October revolution in the USSR. John Lawrence remained unmoved by the hostile press. While the Hungarian uprising was being snuffed out, thousands of East Germans were voting with their feet towards the west and British communists were wrestling with an almost existential crisis, Lawrence was calmly pulling St Pancras closer to Moscow. Was it a coincidence that of all the councils across Britain the burghers of Gera chose to make overtures to St Pancras, now under the leadership of John Lawrence? Perhaps. But the arrangement must have been kept under surveillance by the British security services. It is inconceivable that there are no reports among the papers, which the Home Office still refuses to release.

Nuclear Defence: Labour Splits

While Hungary caused turmoil on the communist left, another even more serious issue emerged with a much wider draw. In 1955, the Tory government announced that Britain would join the arms race and manufacture its own Hydrogen bomb. This, combined with moves to promote West German rearmament as a bulwark against Soviet expansionism in Europe, ratcheted up Cold War tensions. Relationships between the Cold War superpowers were already at rock bottom as experiments with a new generation of nuclear weapons increased – recorded tests rose from around thirty-five in 1956 to over 100 in 1958.

Labour and Conservative leaders were agreed that Britain should maintain its nuclear power status and on the need to develop an independent British H-bomb. It was, after all, the Attlee government which had first given the green light to a British programme with Foreign Secretary Ernest Bevin saying bluntly, 'We've got to have this thing over here whatever it costs and we've got to have the bloody Union Jack flying on top of it.' Controversy then heightened further over the next phase of the nuclear programme. The development of the H-bomb, which was between 1,000 and 1,500 times more powerful that than the atomic bombs dropped on Japan, chilled even an old warhorse like Churchill. Fresh images about the terrible, destructive power of the H-Bomb and its radioactive aftermath sent public anxiety soaring to new heights. Labour and Tory leaders remained more or less united on the need to develop the new weapon but disquiet now became more commonly expressed in the parliamentary Labour Party, as well as among the grass roots and in local Labour parties like St Pancras.

When the critical issue of national defence and the H-bomb came up for debate in the House of Commons it provoked an unexpected but deeply damaging schism on the Labour benches. Official Labour criticism of Tory policy was confined to an amendment calling for greater transparency about the cost of developing an H-Bomb. Neither Prime Minister Churchill nor Labour leader Attlee seemed to want to talk about the *circumstances* under which nuclear weapons might be deployed: would the H-bomb be used only in retaliation to a Russian nuclear strike or might it ever be used in a first strike against conventional forces? The government was silent on the point, and so too was Labour's front bench. Nye Bevan, however, wanted answers. First, Bevan demanded more clarity from Churchill, but then, to the consternation of colleagues, he put his own front bench under pressure. What would Labour do? 'I want my honourable friends the Leaders of the Opposition to answer me ... Do they mean that nuclear weapons will be used with the support of the British Labour movement against any sort of aggression?' Now in full flow, Bevan insisted that 'if we cannot have the lead from them let us give the lead'. But who did Bevan mean by *them*: the government or the Labour leadership? And who did he mean by *us*: the Labour leadership or the Bevanites? It was unclear and in any event, when Attlee came to wind up the debate for Labour, he dealt with Bevan's questions in a characteristically Attlean fashion: he simply ignored them.

Parliamentary convention had it that after Attlee sat down the responsible minister – in this case, Defence Secretary Harold Macmillan – would speak last and close the debate for the government. But Bevan was having none of it. Before Macmillan could rise to the Despatch Box, Bevan leapt to his feet again demanding answers not from the Tories but from his own leader. It was an extraordinary intervention and one of the most dramatic moments of post-war parliamentary history. Attlee ducked and hedged to avoid giving a specific answer about the exact circumstances under which Labour would support a nuclear strike while Bevan sat muttering audibly (and accurately) 'that's no answer, that's no answer'. Attlee, of course, was doing what party leaders do on difficult issues – fudging and trying to hold his party together while Bevan rolled around the parliamentary deck like the loosest of cannons.

Some sixty other Labour MPs, led by Bevan, refused to support Attlee and the official Labour line when it came to the vote. Their mass abstention sparked an almighty row within the Labour Party, which had devastating consequences. Other Labour MPs were outraged by Bevan's behaviour and after a furious meeting of the parliamentary party he had the whip withdrawn. A few days later, Labour's National Executive Committee met to discuss his expulsion and Bevan came within a few votes of being thrown out of the party altogether. The only reason that some on the NEC did not vote for Bevan's expulsion was because they knew it would split Labour – just as the party split in the 1930s, and again later in the 1980s.

This astonishing row between Labour leaders on the floor of the House of Commons clarified nothing yet exposed the deep rift in the party. It looked as though the left-wing Bevanite movement was about to erupt and challenge the party hierarchy all over again. But this time it was different because even among the Bevanites opinions ranged from outright pacifism to support for the official pro-nuclear position articulated by Attlee. Denis Healey subsequently described Labour's views on defence at this time as 'ever more Byzantine' as party leaders struggled to find the right policy to fit the new, awful reality. Not surprisingly, ordinary Labour Party members up and down the country – let alone the wider voting public – were baffled and bewildered by the latest bout of Labour turmoil. Soon after the Commons fiasco, Richard Crossman recorded miserably in his diary that 'by some mischance last night I had to go through the sleet to address a meeting in Epsom, to find twenty-eight shivering Labour Party members waiting in a Co-op hall bewildered – utterly bewildered – and disheartened by the latest row because they really couldn't understand who was standing for what and why anybody was on any side ... I'm afraid that the real fact is that it is now the dispute itself, and not the issues, that people are worrying about.' Many members of the Labour Party today almost certainly feel the same about the renewal of the Trident nuclear weapons system in the twenty-first century. Complex moral and technical issues about the most adequate means of national defence in the modern world have become conflated with debates about what Labour is for and how it should be led.

It is almost as though Labour has suffered from some kind of unfortunate metaphysical time slip.

Civil Defence: St Pancras Makes a Stand

During 1956 the British military began to test a series of massive H-bombs off the Christmas Islands in the Pacific. The results were alarming. After one, the crew of a Japanese fishing boat, ironically named the *Lucky Dragon*, returned to land their catch with radiation sickness so acute that many of them died. When the bomb had been detonated, the vessel was outside the exclusion zone, 85 miles away. Exactly what such a blast might mean if the Russians decided to bomb London was helpfully described by the government's leading nuclear scientist Sir William Penney to a cabinet committee:

> A five megaton bomb hydrogen bomb ... dropped on London and bursting on impact would produce a crater 3/4 of a mile across and 150 feet deep and a fireball of 2 1/4 miles diameter. Suburban houses would be wrecked at a distance of 3 miles of the explosion and they would lose their roofs and be badly blasted at a distance of 7 miles. All habitations would catch fire over a circle of 2 miles from the blast.

Sir William's report was not, of course, made public but it didn't need to be. Enough people were doing their own calculations and speculation was fuelled by a whole raft of films, television series and books about a nuclear exchange and its consequences. Who knew what the end result would be? Certainly not the government. Another highly confidential report in 1955 concluded that 'Hydrogen Bomb war would be total war in a sense not hitherto conceived. The entire nation would be on the front line.'

It was in the context of nuclear tests and Labour's civil war that St Pancras Council decided to take matters into its own hands with a policy initiative which yet again triggered debate around the country. Under the 1948 Civil Defence Act – passed by the Attlee government – all councils had a duty to provide civil defence in the event of an attack. As the immense destructive power of the H-bomb became more apparent, sceptical councillors up and down the country wondered if there would be much left to defend after a nuclear exchange. Some of the St Pancras councillors were among the apprehensive. Over the summer of 1956 they, together with local priests and trade unionists, sponsored a conference on the H-Bomb in St Pancras. One suggestion, swiftly taken up, from the conference was that the council should abandon a 'Civil Defence Week' planned by the Home Office. John Lawrence claimed that the exercise would be '...a complete waste of time and money' and Councillor Clive Jenkins reflected that 'in the sort of world we are going to be living in (after a nuclear attack) there won't be many people left to rescue.' Even under the most benign scenario, a nuclear strike on central London would have flattened areas like St Pancras, leaving little in the way of vital infrastructure or survivors.

The boycott was soon followed by a decision to completely abandon *all* civil defence in the borough. This was a much more serious step than simply opting out of week's civil defence exercises though and put would the councillors beyond the law. When councillors debated the move they were given a formal warning by the town clerk that the resolution was effectively illegal, or *ultra vires*. As a local authority, St Pancras had a legal duty to provide civil defence and the Home Secretary had the power to ensure that the service was continued – at the councillors' personal expense, if the council failed to meet its obligation. The town clerk was instructed to write to the Home Office but there was scarcely any need. Yet again St Pancras hit the headlines. The national press seized on the story and in the battle which ensued between the council and the government over the following weeks the intense media interest continued unabated.

The council based their case for the abolition of Civil Defence on the government's own White Paper, 'Defence: Outline of

Future Policy', which had been published in spring 1957. White Papers are normally statements published by government to help the wider public understand what future policy will be. They are intended to provide clarity and certainty. This White Paper did neither. As Britain entered a new and dangerous phase of the Cold War in the nuclear age, the statement simply revealed the extent of the muddle headed thinking which was guiding the country into uncharted territory. Within a few pages the White Paper managed to describe civil defence as both essential and futile.

Clause 12 read:

> It must be frankly recognised that there is at present no means of adequate protection for the people of this country against the consequences of an attack with nuclear weapons.

This conclusion was then qualified to the point of contradiction by Clause 18, which said:

> While available resources should as far as possible be concentrated on building up an active deterrent power, it would be wrong not to take some precautions to minimise the effect of a nuclear attack, should the deterrent fail to prevent war. Civil Defence must accordingly play an essential part of the defence plan.

Clause 19 added to the confusion by stating that because of spending restraints,

> The main task (now) will be to keep the existing local organisation in being, so as to provide a basis on which realistic planning can continue... These preparations will provide a framework for planning, should that later be necessary.

In his memoirs, Labour's shadow Army Minister George Wigg described the White Paper as 'the most disastrous document published during my Parliamentary life'. St Pancras Council seized gleefully on the contradictions and decided to abandon civil defence altogether, passing a resolution that stated: 'In view of the government's admission in the recent White Paper that there is no real defence against Atom and Hydrogen bomb warfare we are of the opinion that to continue with Civil Defence is a complete waste of public money.' And, it was hoped, 'this action will be followed by similar action from other local authorities so that the government will be impressed with the urgency of abolishing all Atomic and Hydrogen bombs as the only means of preventing the wholesale slaughter of the people in any future wars.'

There followed lengthy correspondence between St Pancras Council and the Home Office as Whitehall officials struggled to draft explanations of how they thought the White Paper should be interpreted. The calibrated Home Office view was set out in a letter sent individually to all councillors. It began by reiterating that the overall defence strategy was based on a deterrence theory of nuclear weapons but that

> It [the White Paper] goes on to state that it would be wrong not to take precautions against the failure of the deterrent to prevent war, so as to minimise the effects of a nuclear attack should it occur, that civil defence must accordingly continue to play an essential part in the defence plan ... The Government is satisfied that should the deterrent fail to prevent war civil defence preparations made in advance would save very many lives that might otherwise be lost, and would do much to provide the framework for an organised society.

Understandably, many councillors were sceptical that there would be much of a framework left following a nuclear attack on central London. After a stormy debate – including an adjournment to eject protesters in the public gallery – the council voted again to abandon civil defence and send an open letter to the Home Secretary explaining why:

We are not, as you suggest, under any misapprehension as to the value of civil defence preparations. The government review of defence referred to in your letter states quite clearly 'that there is no means of providing adequate protection for the people of this country against the consequences of an attack with nuclear weapons ... widespread devastation could not be prevented'. We find it impossible to reconcile this statement with the paragraph in your letter which informs us that 'the Government is satisfied that should the deterrent fail to prevent war civil defence preparations made in advance would save very many lives that might otherwise be lost, and would do much to provide the framework for the preservation of an organised society'.

The council's letter then moved on to critique the entire government defence policy:

When you state that the only means of preventing war is by a race to create thermo-nuclear deterrents we must register a profound disagreement. The last two major wars were each preceded by a fierce competition in arms manufacture accompanied by protestations on all sides that the object was simply to deter aggression and prevent war. Thus were people deceived, and millions of dead in all countries bear witness to the futility of such a policy. As public representatives of the people we have no right to believe, or cause others to believe, that an arms race in this nuclear age would have any other result – except that the scale of mass slaughter and suffering will be even greater.

The letter then asserted – with justification – that British aggression during the Suez debacle of November 1956 had brought the world to the brink of another war and complained that a recent agreement with the USA would allow Britain to become a base for American missiles over which London had no control.

It surely follows that if the USA should become involved in armed conflict with the USSR anywhere in the world – and even if the British Government itself were not directly involved – an immediate target for the Russian hydrogen bombs would be the American rocket bases in this country ... We ask you to reassert the independence of this country by adopting a position of neutrality as between both of the two major world powers. We ask you to remove from these islands those foreign war bases which daily threaten to bring terrible destruction to this country and its people. We ask you to adopt a policy of non-interference in the affairs of other countries, and, finally, we ask you to cease to manufacture and to test thermo-nuclear weapons and, by this example, endeavour to persuade other nations to do likewise ... Unless and until you do this, civil defence preparations are simply war preparations and we cannot participate in them.

By this time, the row between St Pancras Council and the Conservative government was the focus of national attention. The two local MPs joined in and tabled parliamentary questions about the efficacy of civil defence in the event of a nuclear attack; the questions were stonewalled by the Home Secretary who continued to remind the council of its legal obligation. Back in St Pancras, the local civil defence volunteers were also demonstrating their stiff upper lip. Their leader, Tory councillor Tim Donovan, was in a bullish mood when he told the *Daily Mail*: 'We don't care if officially we don't exist. The boys and girls are determined to go on.'

The St Pancras Council Conservative group made one final attempt to break the deadlock in late May 1957 when they tabled emergency resolutions to reinstate civil defence. These were debated at a specially convened meeting of the council meeting which was stormy, wide ranging, and extensively covered in the media. One Tory leader expressed his joy at both civil defence and the British nuclear warheads: 'I am delighted that the Christmas Island tests were conceived. I am delighted that they were carried out and I am delighted that they were a success. Anything which adds strength to our country gives me pleasure.' John Lawrence replied that the national interest was best served by abandoning civil defence and that where St Pancras led others would follow: 'We are convinced that the majority of the Labour movement will support us in this stand and that eventually it will become official Labour policy.'

When it came to a vote the Labour majority voted yet again to abandon civil defence; it was a decisive step into illegality with severe financial consequences. If the council undertook to provide civil defence it could claim a substantial grant, 75 per cent, from central government to help offset the cost. But if it failed to provide the service, the Home Office were empowered to run the service direct and then present the entire bill to the local authority, which would then lose its entitlement to the 75 per cent grant. Those councillors responsible for failing to operate a 'local' service could then be accused by ratepayers of negligence. By failing to take advantage of the grants from central government they would incur unnecessary expenditure on the rates. Ratepayers could then ask for councillors to be surcharged or made personally responsible for the expenditure – estimated to be around £7,000. At the end of May, the Home Secretary simply overrode the council's protest and appointed a commissioner to run civil defence in St Pancras. But the official faced an immediate snag: he had no office and so followed a tussle that could have graced a script from *Dad's Army*. The council quickly earmarked the existing Civil Defence HQ in Camden High Street for conversion to flats, but the Home Office responded by requisitioning the building to try and regain possession. The farrago prompted an unusual protest by John Lawrence, which did more than anything to publicise the council's cause and, according to one witness, it began something like this:

'Why, sir,' said a policeman staring at John Lawrence, 'Who did that to you?'

'Nobody,' said Lawrence, 'I did it myself'.

'But why did you do that, sir?' the simple copper asked.

'I did it as a protest against nuclear weapons,' John simply replied.

The leader of St Pancras Council was chained across the metal doors at the entrance to the civil defence offices in Camden High Street. The new commissioner was due to arrive at any time, but with Lawrence pinned to the doors access would be impossible, which is exactly why he had put himself there. The novel protest was designed more with an eye to the media than any real attempt to block the commissioner and it worked. The coverage was huge and took the confrontation between St Pancras and the government nationwide, although as Peggy Duff recalled, it nearly went horribly wrong.

> I arrived in the High Street to find a small group of John's supporters, including several councillors, parading up and down outside the Civil Defence HQ with suitable banners ... After some time a policeman arrived and plodded up and down the street beside the parades ... Then, when the copper was standing, half asleep, some way up the road, John produced a rather large and ostentatious padlock and chain and attached himself to the bars of the gate. For a time nothing happened. Nobody noticed. Shoppers hurried by and never turned to look. The policeman went on plodding up and down. Buses passed to and fro. No press arrived. There was the leader of the council chained to the gates – and nobody had even turned to look. I had a horrible feeling nobody ever would. Then at last the policeman as he passed saw that something was amiss. He stopped. He stared.

Before long a large crowd, press and more police arrived. Lawrence was eventually released from the gates and sent on his way without being charged. But the point was made. Both the national and provincial press loved the story and images of the Leader of St Pancras Council chained to the gates of the Civil Defence HQ were carried across the nation. Lawrence's protest fuelled a national debate about the merits of civil defence in the nuclear age and in St Pancras town hall he spoke to a large public meeting. The council leader lambasted the money wasted on nuclear arsenals and the futility of trying to defend London against attack, explaining that 'our CD corps consist of wardens with whistles and one telephone box … Civil Defence is a deception of the people and we want no part of it'. Lawrence calculated that the bill for running civil defence in St Pancras, for which councillors would now be liable as individuals, would 'probably be around £7,000' and chuckled 'but we haven't paid it yet'. He was then asked what would happen if the councillors did not pay up. 'If we don't pay,' replied Lawrence, 'the Government comes and takes it out of us somehow. But as we haven't got much which can be taken out of us, presumably we shall have to go to the Scrubs or Pentonville (prison). What I want to know is … if we don't pay up will you back us up?' and at this point the audience roared their support for more than two minutes. These must have been exhilarating moments.

Unfortunately for Lawrence, there was little sign that the enthusiasm extended much beyond his followers gathered in St Pancras town hall. No other council followed the St Pancras lead and it is questionable just how much traction the issue had with Labour voters in the area. Lena Jeger recalled canvassing a block of St Pancras council flats during one election campaign. Wearied by seemingly endless flights of steps and door knocking, she at last reached the top floor, where the door was opened by a hassled mother. Jeger began her election spiel about the need for a Labour government and, in particular, removal of the threat of nuclear weapons. 'Never mind that,' said the woman, 'one of the neighbours keeps pissing in the lift. What you going to do about it?' Jeger murmured sympathetically and ploughed on with her election offer to improve global security by ridding the world of the nuclear menace but was cut short by the woman insisting 'the lift, the lift - what are you going to do about the piss in the lift?' Exasperated, Jeger said that, with the best will in the world, there was probably little she could do about urine in the lift. 'Well if you can't stop people pissing in a lift how the hell are you going to get the Russians and Americans to scrap their nuclear weapons?' And with that, she shut the door.

The story reflects the fact that most people consider sound defence to be one of the few essential duties of government. They are suspicious of overblown promises and uncomfortable when the defence becomes overly politicised or sectarian. Yet this is what happened in St Pancras and the civil defence protest generated another round of negative press comment later in the year when the mayor refused to invite the Civil Defence Corps to the borough's annual Remembrance Day parade. As subsequent leaders of the Labour Party such as Michael Foot and Jeremy Corbyn have discovered, sections of the media will find signs of disrespect on Remembrance Day even where none is intended. The St Pancras Tory leader, Tim Donovan, told the *Daily Mail* that the snub to his 'boys and girls' was 'appallingly bad manners' and the *London Evening News* smelt insult in the air:

> The extreme left wing socialists who control Pancras Borough Council have an unbelievable knack of getting themselves in to the news. Their latest caper is especially graceless ... Let it be conceded that the sentiments of the opponents of civil defence are sincere. But ... the purpose of Remembrance Day ceremonies is to unify and to heal ... [this] extraordinary behaviour [is] quite unworthy of the Labour Party.

Once again, John Lawrence was prepared to follow the relentless logic of his beliefs, even when it put him on the wrong side of public opinion. The presence of the Defence Corps on Remembrance Day would have changed nothing and avoided the reams of bad publicity which was cast over the image of the Labour Party nationally.

By this time, however, St Pancras had alienated not just the Tories and whole sections of the media but, more importantly, the council had failed to attract any significant support within the Labour movement. John Lawrence had said time and again that he expected support from other sections of the Labour movement, and knew it was crucial for the St Pancras protest to succeed. At their meeting on 1 May 1957 the councillors had expressed the hope that their action would 'be followed by similar action by other local authorities so that the government will be impressed with the urgency of abolishing all atomic and hydrogen bombs,' and the local Labour Party recorded receiving encouraging messages of support from all over the country. But none of this was ever translated into action. In the event, not a single council joined St Pancras, which was left to fight on alone.

Worse still, other powerful local authority umbrella groups actively refused either to join the St Pancras Council or offer any real support to their protest. The London County Council – controlled by Labour – replied to a request for support by saying that it wanted its own civil defence activities 'to continue unabated'; it simply did not share St Pancras' view that civil defence was useless. The Association of Metropolitan Corporations took the view 'that law and order in this country are based on the fact that decisions of Parliament are paramount. The Association is continually seeking changes in the law by constitutional means but it cannot support the view that local authorities are entitled to decline to perform statutory duties.' Other organisations were equally clear on the constitutional position: laws made in parliament cannot be challenged by local authorities.

Peggy Duff thought that the problem was one of timing and that 'St Pancras was too late. If it had come out earlier in support of Coventry Council's action, there might have been some hope of a significant group of councils jointly refusing to operate the civil defence services'. Even with greater coordination, however, no other councils were prepared to join the protest and the failure was scarcely just one of timing. The fact was that other local authorities were twice given a lead first by Coventry and then St Pancras. There was no response on either occasion. This was not due to a lack of moral courage. It was simply because they did not agree with the strategy proposed. Respect for the rule of law was an important factor in the isolation of St Pancras, but in the autumn of 1957, there was another shift, a political sea change, which stymied the council's protest over civil defence. The Bevanite challenge of the Labour left to the party establishment was ebbing fast and, ironically, the end came over the issue of nuclear weapons.

Bevan's Bombshell

In September 1957 the Labour Party met at Brighton for its annual conference – a gathering that turned out to be one of the most dramatic in the party's post-war history. Nye Bevan's wife, Jenny Lee MP, set the scene in her memoirs:

> During the summer of 1957 an awareness of all the horrendous consequences that nuclear power could let loose on all of us took possession of the minds and imagination of the active members of the Labour Party as they met to prepare their resolutions for the annual party conference in the autumn. All else was dwarfed by comparison.

The H-bomb tests on Christmas Island left a horrified fascination at the awesome power of nuclear weapons. As local Labour parties up and down the country met over the summer there was one topic above all which they wanted to discuss at the Brighton conference and that was defence – more than 120 resolutions were tabled for discussion at Brighton. Naturally enough, the Holborn and St Pancras South Labour Party submitted a resolution on the threat of nuclear war and civil defence which read: 'This conference recognising that there is no defence against the Hydrogen bomb and that all attempts at Civil Defence tend to create a feeling of false security calls for an end to this deception of the people.'

When conference came to discuss disarmament and foreign affairs the 120 resolutions had been boiled down into just three 'composite' motions (as they are known). Two of the resolutions were fairly innocuous, calling for the immediate end of weapons testing and the phased reduction of nuclear stockpiles to be supervised by an international agency such as the United Nations. But the third resolution went much further. It demanded total unilateralism – i.e. that Britain should simply renounce the ownership and use of all nuclear weapons forthwith. Pacifist in intent, the resolution triggered a destructive, explosive debate which has gone down in the annals of Labour history as a turning point for the party. It was moved by a delegate from south London who argued in a fiery speech that the next Labour government should:

> Stop the tests ... stop the manufacture of the bomb ... renounce the use of the bomb in any war ... [and] give a lead, not only to the Labour movement in this country but to the workers and the working class movement throughout the world for them too to call on their governments to refuse to have anything to do with the hydrogen bomb. We believe that this is the only practical policy.

The resolution's seconder, Harold Davies MP, was even more emotive and pleaded that 'The last child that dies in a radioactive England will curse with the flammule of his breath the movement that had not the courage to give a moral, economic and defence lead to the world'. And so the debate continued, awash with hyperbole and sentiment until the shadow Foreign Secretary rose to wind up the debate on behalf of the party leadership.

Always a master orator, Bevan's speech was fluid and passionate. But it was not what most delegates expected.

Bevan reminded delegates of their impotence in demanding unilateral disarmament because Labour was in opposition – and in opposition it could do nothing; 'You may call that s-s-statesmanship,' said Bevan, using his natural stutter to full oratorical effect, 'But I call it an emotional s-s-spasm'. Amid the jeers and applause Bevan pushed on to argue that if Labour were in government the resolution would be even more damaging because it would commit the party to breaking agreements and treaties with other countries – some of which were socialist, many of which were in the Commonwealth – without any negotiations whatsoever. The resolution would, he said, send him or any other Foreign Secretary, 'naked into the conference chamber' when the best way to diminish the stockpiles of nuclear weapons was to reduce them by negotiations.

According to Jennie Lee, what Bevan said, or perhaps the way he said it, took most of the constituency delegates completely by surprise; they did not like what they heard. After years of enjoying his role as the visionary of the party's left, Bevan stunned the conference by confronting it with this stark political reality and the reaction of the constituency delegates is legendary. Bitter and confused, they rounded on their erstwhile hero. Why this should be so or what they expected is a mystery: perhaps they had forgotten that Bevan had been a member of the Attlee cabinet which had signed off on Britain becoming a nuclear power in the first place.

For the St Pancras rebels, the content and timing of Bevan's volte-face could not have been worse. It left them completely isolated from the new Gaitskell-Bevan axis which sought to project an image of the Labour Party as united, responsible and multi-lateralist. At the council meeting in May, John Lawrence had claimed that St Pancras' policy would be supported by the majority of the Labour movement. The claim was far-fetched, even at the time. After Bevan's speech at Brighton it sounded simply foolish. Lawrence was, like many activists, furious – 'the lion who has lost his mane' was how he dubbed Bevan after Brighton and he was not alone. A few weeks later Bevan went to speak to the conference of the London Labour Party at St Pancras town hall and was shouted down by his former supporters. Disillusioned and disorientated, the Labour left had now had to find another strategy for achieving nuclear disarmament following the rupture with their erstwhile leader. Once again, Holborn and St Pancras was at the centre of a new political development which became a focal point of radical politics for decades to come.

The Birth of Protest Movement CND

The Campaign for Nuclear Disarmament (CND) was founded in February 1958 to galvanise public opinion against nuclear weapons. The first organising secretary was the St Pancras councillor Peggy Duff, and the movement's national offices were in Holborn. Duff recalled the CND as big tent politics bringing together:

> Members of Parliament, professors and students, teachers and schoolchildren, librarians and nurses, actors and printers, entomologists and engineers, philosophers and plumbers, doctors and draughtsmen, firemen and farmers, every possible profession and trade.

CND, she said, had an 'absolutist and compulsive' mission to get rid of nuclear weapons, all of them. It wanted to do it very quickly.

The movement managed to combine a leadership of voices that were listened to – philosopher Bertrand Russell was elected president and Cannon Collins of St Paul's Cathedral elected chair – with numbers which commanded attention. Five thousand people turned up to the first mass meeting in central London. By 1960, over 100,000 people joined CND's annual march between central London and the nuclear research centre at Aldermaston. Many of the protesters were prepared to put their liberty on the line if it came to it: more than 1,100 CND supporters were arrested in September 1961 at a sit-down demo in Trafalgar Square.

CND rapidly moved way beyond Lawrence's lonely, vanguardist protest when he chained himself to the gates of the Civil Defence HQ in Camden High Street. It mobilised numbers for a radical cause that the St Pancras council leader dreamed about but could not match. And yet, oddly, Lawrence was never among them because CND was unilateralist and he was not. Bevan was not a unilateralist and nor was John Lawrence, although they arrived at the same conclusion with different reasoning. Lawrence believed in 'the workers' bomb'. He thought that Britain should keep the bomb because one day it would become a socialist republic, be threatened by the USA, and so need the bomb to defend itself from Washington. The logic was followed by others on the Marxist left at the time who also rejected CND. *Marxism Today* magazine, for example, argued that:

> The question is what policy will unite the greatest number of people to get rid of the bomb. Experience has shown that unilateralism only divides the movement and diverts attention from the real issue, namely international agreement to ban nuclear weapons. This is the only way to banish the menace of nuclear war and also the issue on which the greatest number of people agree.

As 1957 drew to a close, the publicity around St Pancras' civil defence policy slackened and interest in whether the council would continue their defiance was overtaken by other local developments. Early in the summer of 1958, John Lawrence and thirteen other councillors were expelled from the Labour Party (*see* chapter 6). More moderate, less confrontational councillors took control of the St Pancras Council and were forced to make some immediate and humiliating policy U-turns. Decisions were needed quickly on both the civil defence and housing. In both these areas the council had adopted policies that were in breach of the law, with the possible consequence that individual councillors would be forced to pay from their own pockets (surcharged) and disqualified from office. In July 1958, the Home Office presented St Pancras Council with the entire bill – nearly £3,400 – for running civil defence in the borough. Negotiations between the council and the Home Office continued throughout the autumn but it was increasingly evident that councillors would have to resume the organisation of civil defence or face surcharging.

By early November 1958, the new leaders of the Labour group were under enormous pressure to abandon the policy and were being taunted from left and right. Lawrence and the other counsellors expelled from the Labour Party accused them of betrayal. The Conservative opposition were now exploiting the fragmentation on the Labour benches and looking forward to the forthcoming elections due in May 1959 when they had the real prospect of winning the council for the first time in six years. After a rancorous debate, Labour councillors abstained on a Conservative resolution to reinstate civil defence and only the Independent Socialists led by Lawrence voted for continued defiance. Lawrence urged his former colleagues not to be cowed by the threat of surcharging, to hold their ground and to fight. It was typical of an approach that held that any political compromise was 'cant, humbug and hypocrisy'. But by this time the Labour Group was in no mood for an unequal struggle with the District Auditor that would lead, inevitably, to personal surcharge and bankruptcy.

'A real political issue' was how Peggy Duff described the tussle over civil defence and she was right. The proliferation of terrifying new weapons was of huge concern and triggered an almost literally existential debate about their use. The council and the two MPs were quite correct to challenge the government vigorously about the confusion in the White Paper and try to extract honest answers about the role of civil defence. Yet the protest was flawed. Lawrence was right to say that the issue went to the heart of the relationship between central and local government. He was wrong to think that the council was in any position to mount an effective challenge. The council's subsequent claim that it 'cannot see how an appointed person [i.e. the commissioner appointed by the Home Office] can continue to carry out duties in the name of an elected council which has refused to do them' was simply naive posturing. The vanguardist tactics left St Pancras looking isolated rather than principled. Most other councils – including many controlled by Labour – came to the conclusion that the Tory government had legal force and a democratic majority behind it. Then, with Bevan's 'naked into the conference chamber' speech of 1957, there was a transformation within Labour, after which the ousting of the Tory government in Westminster became the primary objective. Yet the attempt at unity was too little and too late. When the general election came in 1959, Macmillan increased his majority and Labour's fragile unity over defence policy disintegrated.

In 1960 the Labour Party conference at Scarborough approved a resolution which committed the party to unilateral nuclear disarmament. By then Bevan was dead and there was no one of his stature or with his credibility to put the case against. Labour leader Hugh Gaitskell put the party on notice that he would ignore the resolution and 'fight, fight and fight again to save the party we love'. Gaitskell never had any intention of being bound by the conference decision but it is often forgotten that he was not arguing for the retention of an independent British nuclear weapons. He was simply arguing for continued membership of NATO under the US nuclear umbrella until such time as there was a multilateral agreement to end all nuclear weapons. Gaitskell's vision has never materialised but no Labour prime minister since has ever come close to renouncing an independent British nuclear deterrent.

Far from it. Nevertheless, in the late 1950s the debates and the marches went on. Aldermaston, Trafalgar Square and the mass demonstrations of CND mobilised large numbers of people understandably apprehensive about the future. Many other people, however, struggled with a daily concern that was literally closer to home: where were they going to live?

Chapter 5

RENTS, RATS AND RACHMAN

'Tory talk about a property owning democracy is all bunk. One of the best examples of a property owning democracy is our great co-operative movement.'

Clement Attlee, Labour Prime Minister 1945–51

'The Rent Act of 1957 probably caused more misery to ordinary working people than any other piece of Conservative legislation in the 1950s.'

Michael Stewart, Labour MP and former Foreign Secretary

'Young couple with baby daughter desperately seeking …', 'young English couple urgently require …', 'couple willing to do decoration …' Small ads like these in local newspapers of the 1950s tell their own tales in a pathetic line or two and hint at countless individual stories of despair. Without doubt, the biggest headache for many in post-war London remained finding a decent place to live. Immediately after the war, Labour had kicked off a massive building programme led by local councils and supported by central government (*see* Chapter 1). This was not the Tory approach, which became evermore dependent on the laissez-faire ideals of the free market to solve Britain's housing crisis – several of the Tory housing ministers who piloted the policies later became pioneers of Thatcherism. From 1951 onwards, commercial speculators took centre stage in various roles, either developing offices or building for owner occupiers or as landlords in the private rented sector. St Pancras, like other councils, tried to push back against powerful market forces and the increasingly tight financial constraints set by national government: slum clearance, rebuilding after the Blitz and the provision of good housing at affordable rents remained their priorities. These two competing visions of housing – as a tradeable commodity like any other or as an indispensable bedrock of healthy communities – laid the foundations for a political clash, which led to the St Pancras riots.

Living in Limbo: Requisitioned Tenants

The first of the Tory measures to hit central London was the Requisitioned Houses Act (1955), which abolished the powers of local councils to take over – or requisition – empty property. The Act is almost forgotten now but was hugely important during and just after the Second World War. During the war, when wealthy owners of big townhouses frequently fled to the country for safety, local councils were allowed to requisition the empty property. The procedure itself was straightforward: a local authority simply needed to issue a requisition notice and send someone round with a hammer and nail to pin it to the front door of the property. The owners then had a week or so to move back in themselves or lose control of the building. In the collectivist, 'all in it together' spirit of wartime London, this drastic action was accepted. On just one day, for example, St Pancras' borough surveyor requisitioned fifty large houses in Bloomsbury to provide temporary shelter for families made homeless by the Blitz. In Holborn, the indefatigable Labour leader of the post-war council, Ina Chaplin, went round in person to hammer in the nails and requisition the houses (*see* chapter 9). The spacious properties on middle-class residential estates, such as those in Bloomsbury, became what local MP Lena Jeger described as 'an essential part' of the London housing stock and, even a decade after the war's end, there were still tens of thousands of families living in requisitioned houses.

But, as the country recovered after the war, the use of requisitioning as a solution to the housing shortage was cut back. Quite understandably, many small landlords wanted their properties back to live in themselves and tens of thousands of houses were handed back to their original owners in the decade after the end of the war. The 1955 Act said that local authorities that had requisitioned houses should return all properties to their owners by 1960. For some local councils this created yet another housing dilemma because families living in the properties would need rehousing and even as late as 1958 there were still 28,000 requisitioned properties left around the country. Of these 90 per cent were in London – with more than 800 in St Pancras. Moreover, the majority of the remaining requisitioned houses were by now in the hands of speculators. They had bought up the properties with sitting tenants, cheaply, and were now anxious to clear out the occupants and cash in their investment.

The new Conservative housing minister, Duncan Sandys, and his parliamentary aid Enoch Powell apparently believed that many of the sitting tenants would be allowed to remain when the houses were returned to private landlords. Lena Jeger understood the London housing market better and in a Commons debate she warned of the consequences:

> Why [Conservatives] should imagine that, instead of letting these houses with bits of furniture at the rate of two or three guineas per room per week, landlords are to keep the council tenants as statutory tenants at controlled rents, I simply cannot understand. It must be due to their lack of experience of landlords in London.

At that time, St Pancras already had thousands of families on their waiting list for rehousing. The addition of another 800 families living in buildings which were about to be derequisitioned from council control and returned to the private sector would make a bad situation worse. Jeger argued that:

> What this Bill really says to us is that for years and years there must be a standstill on our waiting lists. We have got to turn all our new accommodation to meeting this problem. We are put in a position where we will never be able to get people out of damp basements, often where we have children coming into dangerous contact with tuberculosis. All we get is a Bill which is completely a landlord's Bill.

The forecast turned out to be uncannily accurate. Between 1956 and 1959 the numbers of people waiting on the St Pancras housing list rose from 5,483 to 6,329 – an increase of just over 800, pretty much as Jeger had predicted. Many councils tried to avoid this extra pressure and were reluctant to derequisition properties because they had nowhere to rehouse the tenants. Labour were wholly opposed to derequisitioning and argued that it did not make sense when there was already an acute crisis in housing. As Peggy Duff recalled:

> There seemed no justice at all in handing back these houses to their owners together with the tenants who would lose their security ... We would have preferred additional powers to requisition empty houses – a fine hope even with a Labour Government, much less with the Tories in power. But the law is the law and reluctantly, at the last possible moment, we handed back the houses we held.

Paying for the 'Blast of War'

A year later, in 1956, Sandys slashed the amount of subsidies and cheap loans available for local authority housing programmes. Labour had given generous central government grants to local authorities for all housebuilding but the Tory government cut back this support. Under the new law, local councils could claim central government help for housing particular groups such as the elderly and slum clearance. Any other council building would have to be paid for out of existing council tenant rental income, the rates – the local tax levied by councils – or by borrowing on the open market. (Perversely, Sandys' subsides encouraged the building of tower blocks or 'streets in the sky' as they were euphemistically called; and so was born a whole new range of social problems.)

The new rules put a big strain on local councils. Central London was especially hard-hit because there would no longer be government help for local authorities trying to make good damage from the Blitz, which still marked much of the city. In Holborn, for example, of 650 homes destroyed during the war only 266 had been replaced. Labour argued that these were national problems which required national funding and that local councils should not be abandoned and left to clear up the mess of the war alone. Once again, Lena Jeger was at the forefront of MPs pressing for changes to the Bill and she tore into the Tory housing minister:

> Frankly, I cannot understand his lack of sympathy, particularly towards areas in London and other big cities which took the full blast of the war ... I should have thought that it would not have been beyond the sympathies of the [Conservatives] to try and help in the rebuilding of those areas which have suffered so much...

Duncan Sandys insisted that rebuilding was a matter for each individual local council but Jeger was having none of it. 'In that case he is saying that the local authority which has already suffered most from the war must now, out of the pockets of its own ratepayers, make good what was a national disaster.' The new law effectively meant that residents of the Tory-voting shire counties could avoid much of the future expense needed to make good the war damage and that more of the costs would be shouldered by inner-city Labour councils. It was, as Jeger complained, anything but fair because 'it was no fault of the people in one district that more of their homes were destroyed than the homes of people anywhere else – I should have thought that would have been a good reason for the Government to have poured help into such a district'.

Slum clearance was still eligible for subsidies under the new rules but even here there was a hitch. The new law's definition of what constituted a slum was now so narrow, said Lena Jeger, 'that there are large numbers of dwellings which do not qualify [for subsidy], although in human terminology they are slums and should be written off as slums'. Pressing home the point, she described the homes of some of her constituents who were living at the fag end of the capital's 'affluent society':

> In them a family lives in one room, washing drying above the heads of the family as they eat their supper, coal in the box next to the table off which they are eating, children having to move their homework off the table because the mother wants to do the ironing. A woman living in such circumstances has to take her children out for a walk on a snowy day so that her husband who is on night duty can get some quiet in order to sleep. Then there is the misery of shared lavatories, of the shared tap on the landing, the shared sink, the one gas cooker in the house which many women must share.

In Holborn, said Jeger, there were entire tenement blocks which 'would have been a disgrace to this country 100 years ago'. Yet just thirty-six were classified as slums. As a consequence, Holborn council could not claim the subsidy for replacing many of the dilapidated buildings or include them in the slum clearance programme. The LCC was similarly hampered by the tight definition of what constituted a slum. The authority had 165,000 families on its waiting list for rehousing with around a third – 50,000 – classed as priority. Yet the LCC could only categorise 18,500 houses as slums and so get help from central government to replace them.

Not surprisingly, substandard housing had an effect on people's health and Jeger vented her frustration at being unable to help those who came to her surgeries. 'What can we do for these people many of whom come to us sick and disabled?' she asked. 'They bring their hopeless pathetic medical certificates which we can only pass on.' And once again she was indignant at the Tories' lack of patriotism and concern for those who had given most in the war. 'Many of them are ex-servicemen who are the most bitter of all. People living in basements with rising damp come to us with their complaints. We can take their addresses, contact the Medical Officer of Health, but time after time, we find that these buildings are not represented as slums.'

The slum landlords which Jeger complained about could be prosecuted under public health laws. At least in theory. In practice, a council's lack of real clout to pursue rogue landlords was spelled out by St Pancras council leader John Lawrence in a speech to the Labour Party Conference of 1957. 'I am on a local authority,' said Lawrence, 'And I can tell you that our sanitary inspector spends most of the time chasing rats and landlords in and out of broken lavatories. In the street next to mine we have prosecuted a landlord twenty-one times in the last two years. Twenty-one times we have hauled him up in front of the court ... and they still do not make repairs.' Far more cases of the type Lawrence was talking about did come to light but not until years later and as a result of the Tories' next piece of housing legislation, the 1957 Rent Act.

The Rent Act and Rachmanism

While cuts to building subsidies and forced derequisitioning piled pressure on local council housing programmes, it was this law – the Rent Act – that did the real damage to the prospect of affordable homes in the capital. London Labour MP and future Foreign Secretary Michael Stewart later reflected that this law 'probably caused more misery to ordinary working people than any other piece of Conservative legislation in the 1950s'.

The 1957 Rent Act set about dealing with these private sector homes which were a critical, if dilapidated, part of Britain's housing stock. Even as late as 1962 there were around 4.5 million privately rented unfurnished homes in Britain and many lacked basic amenities – over half lacked a bath or running hot water supply. The central aim of the Rent Act was to bring market forces to bear on the private rented sector; according to Tory theory, these same forces would increase both the quantity and quality of housing, and solve London's housing crisis. In practice, the Act had catastrophic consequences. Almost overnight, hundreds of thousands of tenants lost their security of tenure (their legal right to remain), a provision which was intended to 'free up the market'. Then the cap on rents was effectively lifted with the predictable effect that rents rocketed skywards due to the shortage of housing supply and at a time of high demand. Only the humblest of households (those living in a house with a rateable value of less than £40) were left with any kind of statutory protection – but even this ended when the existing tenants, or 'stats' as they were known, moved on or died. Predictably, ruthless landlords soon developed methods to make the 'stats' do one or the other. The same run-down properties could then be packed out with many more new tenants, often immigrants or prostitutes, paying much higher market rents.

The full horror of the consequences of the Act was not fully exposed until years later. In 1963, one of the most egregious slum landlords, Perec Rachman, was exposed for the violent intimidation which he used to oust poor but protected tenants from his properties in the Paddington district of London and a new word entered into the English language: Rachmanism. It is defined by *Collins English Dictionary* as 'the extortion or exploitation by a landlord of ... slum property ... especially when involving intimidation to drive out sitting tenants', but the more memorable description came from Labour leader Harold Wilson. 'Sometimes,' said Wilson in a furious Commons speech about Rachman and the housing crisis, 'One turns over a stone in a garden or field and sees the slimy creatures which live under its protection ... But the photophobic animal world has nothing to compare with the revolting creatures of London's underworld, living there, shunning the light, growing fat by battening on human misery'.

Ben Parkin, the Labour MP for Paddington, next to St Pancras, and one of the unsung heroes of post-war politics. Despite threats, he pursued and exposed Rachman after years of painstaking investigation. He explained how Rachman used the 1957 Rent Act to extract the last penny from tenants. And he exposed the flaws in Companies legislation which allowed Rachman and others to avoid paying tax. In his memoirs, Labour MP George Wigg described the research put together by Parkin as 'one of the most moving social documents of our time'. Investigative teams from the BBC's *Panorama* and the *Sunday Times* then followed up to uncover a kind of thuggish modus operandi that would not have been out of place in a Henry Fielding novel about London 200 years before: vulnerable tenants in the properties bought up by Rachman were intimidated out of their homes by beatings, Alsatian dogs or broken sewage pipes left unrepaired for weeks or months.

The real culprit, however, was the Tory government and free market dogma. Rachmanite landlords were doing little that ministers had not been warned about, or actually knew about or ought to have predicted. In the Commons, Wilson pinned the political blame for the Rachman scandal squarely on housing ministers. Campaigners led by Parkin had lobbied in Parliament but their complaints fell on deaf ears. 'They had,' said Wilson, 'about as much impact on the complacency of [ministers] as if they had been describing the housing conditions in Nero's Rome.' Ministers past and present had simply turned a deaf ear so that 'at the Rachman headquarters, if we could ever find them, there must surely be honoured places for portraits of a Macmillan, a Sandys, a Brooke, a [Charles] Hill and a [Sir Keith] Joseph'. George Wigg agreed and later wrote: 'the charge against the government was that they deliberately disregarded the truth and, in so doing, sacrificed the health and happiness of ordinary citizens to maintain the market economy in housing'. Worse still, the housing market created by the Tories was not free, open or transparent.

'If we could ever find them ...' was a crucial phrase in Wilson's speech about the headquarters of Rachman's empire. Like other market operators then and now, Rachman made aggressive use of loopholes in company legislation to avoid penalties and tax. He established such a bewildering array of interlocking companies with nominee owners (i.e. frontmen) that it became almost impossible to work out who owned what. Profits in his empire simply vanished and so tax liability was whittled down to a bare minimum as layers of intermediate companies were paid for fictitious services. (The use of interlocking companies to avoid tax was a scam going on all over the country and one that set alarm bells ringing in the Treasury: between 1955 and 1960 the number of registered companies doubled without, of course, any matching increase in productive output.) When inspectors or a court ordered repairs to, for instance, drainage or sewage of a property, it simply slipped into the ownership of another company, forcing proceedings to start over again. It was a problem that John Lawrence had complained about in his speech to Labour Party conference in 1957 and it became worse in subsequent years.

It did not take long for the tremors caused by the 1957 Rent Act, which dealt with the private sector, to shake public sector housing. First, it created an increased demand for council houses as poorer people were forced out of their homes and sought refuge in local authority housing. Second, as the general level of rents took off, the Act created a new yardstick of what could be taken as an 'economic rent'. This made the task of keeping down council rents almost impossible because if private sector rents rose rapidly public sector rents would need to be kept in line.

Pay Up or Get Out

From the moment the proposals became public, the effect the new law would have was obvious. The local newspaper in St Pancras summed it up in one headline: 'Rent Bill will hit Islington and St Pancras hardest' – central London worst affected. Lena Jeger described the proposed legislation as 'evil' and warned that 'People in central London are bound to suffer harshly ... up to 4 million tenants who will have to "pay up or get out".' It was estimated that around a third of the 34,000 private tenants in Holborn and St Pancras would have to pay hefty increases from decontrolled rents – some rents would more than double – while tenants lost any security of tenure. In addition, the threshold of £40 rateable value put in place to protect the poorest could be abolished at any time under the proposals so that all rents, for even the most basic flats, could be decontrolled in the future.

It was little wonder that Jeger said her mailbag bulged with letters from tenants 'terrified' at the prospect of rent demands which they could not pay. The Labour Party orchestrated a national campaign against the new law in which the local parties, tenants' associations and trade unions of Holborn and St Pancras played an important part. They organised a 10,000-signature petition, which was presented in the House of Commons in March 1957. The petition highlighted St Pancras council's already lengthy waiting list and 'increasingly desperate and difficult' living conditions of local people. Rather than market forces, the petitioners asked for a 'housing programme to provide reasonable homes at rents that people who most need the homes can afford', based on adequate subsidies, low-interest loans for the council's housing programme, powers for the council to requisition properties and the retention of rent controls.

Queues of worried tenants formed outside St Pancras town hall when the Rent Act came into force in July 1957. Councillor and architect David Goldhill – himself facing a stiff rent increase – became the borough's unpaid Rent Act advisor to help deal with the stream of panicked tenants looking for help and information.

The Holborn and St Pancras Labour Party, like others in the capital, opened an advice centre three nights a week with members of the socialist Law Society on hand to advise worried callers. In reality, the council had virtually no powers to help private tenants other than inform them of their minimal rights.

The Tories remained unmoved by the petitions and protests. As the Bill was progressing through parliament, Duncan Sandys' parliamentary aide, Sir Henry Joseph d'Avigdor-Goldsmid MP, penned an article in a local north London newspaper that accused Labour of 'disgraceful scaremongering' about the effects of the new law. Just how much Sir Henry really grasped or cared about the effect of the new law or areas like Holborn and St Pancras though can only be guessed at. Descended from a long line of bankers and bullion brokers, the old Harrovian 2nd Baronet Sir Harry's family home was a Grade I-listed Jacobean mansion in Kent.

Other Tories never did seem to get the point. As evidence mounted about the Rent Act in the early 1960s, the Tory Housing minister was, by pure coincidence, another old Harrovian baronet, Sir Keith Joseph. Labour shadow minister George Wigg recalled that Joseph's understanding of housing 'defied satire as well as sanity'. Joseph denied that the scandals were a product of the free-market Rent Act, and insisted that they were caused by the previous policy of rent control. Wigg said, 'I would be surprised if, even now, Joseph understands that the 1957 Rent Act was an important factor in the pollution of our environment, which has become, perhaps, the most pervasive and intractable of Britain's human problems'. Sir Keith became Mrs Thatcher's free-market guru in the 1970s and had much bearing on social policy – or the lack of it – in the 1980s.

Turning the Clock Back

Could Labour have taken a tougher stand against the Rent Act? Looking back on the period, Michael Stewart (the then Shadow Housing Minister) certainly thought so. He blamed Labour, the church and the press for not having campaigned even more vigorously against the law. But the Tory policy was cast and ministers unflinching despite the opposition inside and outside parliament. Where Labour can perhaps be criticised is for not having a more thought-out, credible policy in opposition. The party's alternative to the market rents in the private sector was a policy of 'municipalisation', although quite how this would work in practice was never spelt out. Labour Party infighting and personality clashes during the 1950s had a high opportunity cost in terms of producing a coherent and agreed policy on a range of issues, and housing was no exception (*see* Chapter 2)

Differences over what to do about Britain's housing crisis were laid bare at Labour's conference at Brighton in the autumn of 1957. All sides agreed that the Rent Act was an iniquity, but how should Labour oppose it? Alice Bacon MP, a long-standing member of the National Executive Committee, proposed an emergency resolution on behalf of the Labour leadership. She stressed that housing 'was a most important debate, one of the most important debates we shall have this week, because this resolution affects the lives of millions of people in this country'. Bacon committed a Labour government to reintroduce security of tenure to give tenants greater control. But she did not promise a return to the old level of rents and spoke merely about protecting tenants from unreasonable rents by giving tribunals the power to fix fair rents. This, Bacon explained, was because Labour accepted that landlords needed extra income to pay for repairs to run-down properties. She recognised that Labour's housing policy had to reflect political reality and told delegates that 'we cannot put the clock back'.

None of this satisfied St Pancras council leader John Lawrence, who was also at the conference. Speaking from the floor, he rose to launch a scathing attack aimed, as so often, as much at Labour's leaders as on the landlords or the Tories: 'Alice Bacon said that we cannot put the clock back. Why can't we put the clock back?' he asked. 'Why can't we repeal the Rent Act and put rents back to where they were before. There is nothing wrong with putting the clock back when the clock is wrong ... What would you say to the tenants who are being worried out of their lives and asked for an extra £1 or 30s for the dirty rat-ridden hovels where I am living?' Lawrence dismissed Bacon's proposal to fix future rents by a tribunal and went on to propose that tenants even be compensated for the higher rents which they had already paid: 'I am not being facetious. I am deadly serious about this. I would suggest that you deduct from future rents all the increases you have paid ... if you repeal something you repeal it all ... It is a war between the landlords and the tenants. Let us, in this conference, show that we are on the side of the tenants.'

Back in St Pancras, Lawrence stepped up the bellicose rhetoric and called repeatedly for direct and if necessary illegal action. He recalled the Glasgow rent strikes of 1915, when women in the city refused to pay increases, and mooted the idea of something similar in St Pancras. At one meeting he argued that 'A mass rent strike is the only answer to this problem – if everybody stands together on this issue there can be no question of mass eviction.' On another occasion he told a crowd that tenants should be prepared to resist evictions physically and that 'no man could possibly take his wife and children into the street in 1957. So don't. Stay put and don't move.'

Lawrence's approach set a tone for the debate which reverberated throughout the borough. Two points became clear. First, the struggle over rents would be seen through the prism of class war – a war, as he put it, between capital and labour represented by landlords and tenants. Secondly, this battle would be taken beyond the normal democratic forums – parliament or the council chamber – for settling disputes. In St Pancras at least, this war was going to be fought out on the streets. Over the next two years it was a call which resonated as much with council tenants as with private tenants in the borough. And it had consequences which even Lawrence could not have then anticipated.

Opposition to the 1957 Rent Act spawned a new umbrella organisation called the Holborn and St Pancras United Workers and Tenants Committees (UWTC) which played a crucial role in the events to come. It harnessed the energies of tenants and trade unionists, communists and Labour Party members. During the first few months of 1957 this group mobilised tenants, helped set up tenants' associations and organised a march to the Hampstead home of Henry Brooke MP, who had just replaced Duncan Sandys as housing minister. Other local tenants' organisations sprang up too.

But not everyone was happy about the role being taken by the UWTC. Many in the Labour Party eyed the organisation with suspicion as little more than a front for the Communist Party. For Labour the UWTC posed similar challenges to those of the pre-war 'Popular Front' or post-war 'Peace Committees' – platforms that harnessed the energy of social democrats but which were effectively steered by communists to push a revolutionary agenda. Eyebrows were raised when Labour council leader John Lawrence appeared alongside Jock Nicholson, the Communist Party's prospective parliamentary candidate for St Pancras North at one UWTC rally. Meanwhile the actual Labour MP for St Pancras North, Kenneth Robinson, distanced himself from Lawrence's comments about rent strikes and told another tenants' meeting that he would not encourage that type of direct action. Just a few weeks later, these tensions within the local Labour Party about how to oppose the Rent Act developed into a full blown split.

Riot at Holborn Hall

One evening in February 1958, some 500 people made their way through the winter fog to Holborn Hall. Heavy with cigarette smoke and noisy chatter, the hall was packed with an impatient crowd. The new housing minister, Henry Brooke, was due to address them and talk about the Rent Act. Even before he arrived, leaflets had been distributed describing Brooke as the 'Minister for Evictions'. Balloons hung lazily around the ceiling with streamers hanging from them with slogans such as 'Evict Henry' or 'Resign'. Despite this, the minister arrived, confident and smiling breezily, although it soon became clear that most of the audience had already made up their minds about what he was going to say and they did not like it. As Brooke began to speak they began to howl, chant and stamp their feet. The confusion was compounded by a group of fascists which had turned up to the meeting and now began to shower the auditorium with pamphlets headed 'Mosley or Slump'.

Brooke struggled on for some minutes before concluding with an offer to answer any questions if the crowd was prepared to sit and listen quietly. But this was not to be. The gangway in front of the platform was quickly congested with people shouting questions and waving pamphlets. Other tenants began to advance menacingly toward the platform and before long there was complete chaos in the hall. John Lawrence, inevitably, emerged on the platform to finish the meeting in a scene described by *The Times*:

> 'The Tory meeting has finished' he [Lawrence] shouted through the din, 'I'm the leader of St Pancras Borough Council ...,' But he too was interrupted and a minute or two later fell off the stage with three policemen who had belatedly arrived from the station over the road. However, cries of 'we want Lawrence' were taken up and he was back again a minute or so later, standing on the table and this time bellowing 'fellow workers, citizens ... We have won this fight against the Tories' but he got no further this time either and was hustled off by the police again. 'The meeting's finished,' a police officer announced, and the hall gradually cleared.

The Holborn Hall riot attracted massive press coverage, almost all of it hostile to those who had triggered the disturbances. *The Times* thought it 'surprising' that no one was arrested. Peggy Duff thought it lucky that no one got hurt. And Henry Brooke said it was a warning to the rest of the country of how things would turn out if the communists or fascists took control. Lena Jeger felt obliged to offer the minister a backhanded apology for the behaviour of her local Labour Party members on the floor of the House of Commons a week later: 'I wish to express my regret at the occurrences at the meeting – I do so because I feel that the arguments against this vicious piece of legislation [the Rent Act] do not need balloons and bicycle chains to underline them.'

Of all the many comments made in the aftermath of the meeting, however, perhaps the most incisive comment came from the *Yorkshire Evening Post*, which said that,

> Nothing could have been more preposterous than the remarks of Councillor John Lawrence as he harangued the audience at Holborn Hall last night: 'the Tories have been forced to go home, we have won the fight.' The fight of course has been won in Parliament. The Bill ... is on the statute book.'

The conclusion was, however regrettable, undeniably true.

A Borough Owned by its People

For London councils like St Pancras, the 1957 Rent Act added significantly to their woes. It created an entirely new yardstick by which to measure a 'fair rent'. In addition to the loss of subsidies, it created a new and unwelcome context in which to try and sustain a housing programme. St Pancras councillors responded with a two-pronged strategy. First, they tried to increase the supply of housing by building more homes, even if that meant building was financed by borrowing on the open market. Secondly, they tried to ensure that rents remained affordable for the tenants. It was a policy that came under pressure from all sides as London began to boom. The rapidly expanding commercial sector in the neighbouring City of London meant that land values and building costs spiralled in St Pancras too. Then, as private sector rents began to rise rapidly the gap between them and council rents, which were pegged, became ever wider and more difficult to justify. Finally, the council lost revenue income from the rates following further changes to local government funding. The conditions created a perfect storm as council spending on housing began to outpace income. Eventually, the district auditor (the central government watchdog over council spending) intervened. When he warned councillors that the housing policy was effectively leading the authority to bankruptcy – for which the councillors would be personally and individually liable – the Labour group split into two irreconcilable factions.

St Pancras was among the leading local authorities in the country in terms of housebuilding. According to government statistics which compared the records of metropolitan boroughs in England and Wales, St Pancras had been the seventh largest builder since the war and had the third largest number of buildings under construction. It was a record to be proud of, but not one that was going to be easily sustained. Despite the hostility of central government policy, St Pancras' Labour council refused to cut back on their ambitious house-building programme. And expansion was rapid. By June 1958, nearly 3,000 new units had been completed since the war, another 1,000 more new homes were part-built and, on the basis of plans already formulated, the council envisaged that the number of new units would rise to over 8,000 by the early 1960s.

In addition to the new building, the council bought up property wherever it could. The most ambitious transaction was the purchase of 851 houses from the Oxford College, Christchurch in 1955. The college wanted to unwind its residential property portfolio in favour of more lucrative investments and St Pancras Council, which at that time could still reclaim 75 per cent of the cost in government grants, willingly took the crumbling estate off the college's hands. Council officers were instructed to look out for any soundly built property which could be purchased and used to alleviate the housing shortage. Between June 1955 and May 1957 St Pancras spent £610,000 on buying up about 1,000 houses and 'municipalising' or taking over 1,670 private tenancies.

But there were limits to what the class-ridden British society would tolerate. When St Pancras Council tried to buy up some of the Grade-I listed terraces that overlook Regent's Park, designed by the pioneering eighteenth-century architect John Nash there was uproar. The elegant Regency edifices, owned by the Crown Commissioners, had been empty for several years and there were plans afoot to demolish them. The commissioners, who were in cahoots with some speculators, only abandoned the plan after a public outcry. But what to do with the 150-year-old terraces? St Pancras Council stepped forward with an offer to buy the crumbling buildings, renovate them and rehouse 120 homeless families. In a more rational era, less bonded to status and privilege, the offer would have been seen as an imaginative, audacious plan. But post-war Britain was not yet that place and social attitudes remained rooted more in Nash's epoch.

Some objected to the paraphernalia of family life like prams and pushchairs being allowed to clutter up the hallways. Others were horrified by the type of people who might come to live in the terraces. The *London Chronicle* opined that the terraces should only be used by people 'who could afford to live elegantly. If it is the will of the people that such folk should be annihilated, then we had best call in the Soviet Secret Police here and now.' In 1960, a rising Tory MP and his film-star wife moved into one of the refurbished flats, No. 3 Chester Terrace. No doubt, John Profumo and Valerie Hobson would have passed the *Chronicle*'s 'elegance' test with flying colours but there was, of course, just one problem. When the philandering Profumo lied to the House of Commons about the casual sex he had enjoyed with a working class teenager young enough to be his daughter, it triggered a scandal that probably did more than any other event of the post-war era to blow open the idea that there was a superior class of people entitled to live in places like Chester Terrace. The fact that the girl, Christine Keeler, was mistress of the racketeer landlord Perec Rachman, who made his fortune by exploiting the poor in his less than elegant Notting Hill slums, just added to the irony.

Undeterred by the rebuff over the Nash terraces, Housing Chair Peggy Duff made it clear that the acquisitions policy would continue. She insisted that even without support from the exchequer 'we'll save as many houses as we can. We will repair them so that they don't fall down. Then they will be converted. If we have our way this borough will be owned by its people.' It was a noble aim but with ever decreasing support from central government it would be increasingly difficult to fulfil.

What is a Fair Rent?

As central government support for local authority housing programmes was scaled down, councils like St Pancras faced a serious dilemma. How could ambitious housing programmes now be financed without steep increases in rent from existing tenants? Household incomes were rising but would this lead to greater equality or simply the payment of higher rents? Generating revenue and finding the right level of rent for tenants remained a tricky problem.

Various rent schemes had been tried in the borough since the war. The 1949–53 Conservative administration set different levels of rent, depending on the type of flat or house and the estate which it was on: the old pre-war houses had the lowest rents, while tenants of newly built flats paid more. But this soon led to social segregation with the better off living on the newer estates and the worst off being herded into sink estates. After 1953 Labour tried a different solution though, as Peggy Duff confessed, it was not wholly successful.

A new scheme was introduced for the new, horrible barrack-type structure being completed on the Regents Park Estate ... The principle was the higher the flat, the higher the rent. The rent went up by two shillings each floor. So, in an eleven-storied block, the tenants on the top floor paid £1 more than those on the ground floor.

But high-rises did not mean better or, as the council soon discovered, more popular. Duff concluded sadly, 'Now that tall blocks are so unpopular, it seems a ludicrous scheme.'

In 1956, the new Labour administration under John Lawrence tried yet another approach. The graded increase of 2s per floor was abolished and rents equalised at the lowest rate. This meant that some tenants got a rent reduction of £1 a week if they lived on the top floor of a tall block, and many others had substantial reductions too. 'Council to Slash Rents' ran the local press headline and according to Duff, 'this was a momentous occasion'. It was probably the last time a council in Britain actually lowered rents. Naturally, the Tories were furious. Tackling inequality was an important part of the reasoning behind the plan and in 1956 the council pressed on with the new low-rent scheme. Duff claimed that the existing rents needed to be lowered because although they were within reach of 60 per cent of the population they were too high for the other 40 per cent. She was quick to blame the Tory central government for creating the problem. 'We believe in building as many new flats as planned despite the Tory Government's reduction in subsidy and we believe that the flats should be provided at costs that people can afford.'

The new policy quickly threw up a dilemma: the council's ambitious building programme was costly and, as central government grants were cut, it was increasingly funded by borrowing on the open market. These loans were repaid from the Housing Revenue Account (HRA) – income collected from tenants' rents. Lower rents meant less cash in the HRA with which to repay the building loans or service debt interest and was a gap that could only be plugged with cash transfers from the council's general income (the rates) into the HRA. It was common for councils to use some of their income from the rates to subsidise their home-building programme because council housing was regarded still as a merit good with important social benefits. But there were legal limits to this subsidy from the rates, as St Pancras Council would find out.

The new low-rent scheme was expensive and would need an ever larger subsidy from the rates revenue. The gap to be plugged between rental income and expenditure on new building would rise very sharply if all the thousands of planned new homes were completed by 1966. Local Tories argued that cheap rents were an unfair burden on those people who would have to help pay the subsidy from their rates but who were not council tenants; they protested loudly that the council had embarked on a course 'of sheer, naked bankruptcy ... with great sums of money being sacrificed on the altar of housing policy'.

Labour retorted that the ballooning deficit was no fault of the low rents or tenants. In 1954, for example, there was a £6,000 surplus on the Housing Revenue Account – in other words, the council had actually made a profit out of its tenants. The reason for the surging deficit now was threefold: the spiralling cost of land in central London as a result of property speculation, the withdrawal of government subsidies and the increased costs of borrowing. The consequence was that in just over a year from 1955 the housing deficit tripled from £30,000 to over £90,000. By 1960, it was estimated that the deficit would be £300,000. Labour flatly rejected the argument that the deficit was down to cheap rents and identified ever-rising costs in London as the real problem. According to one calculation it cost an average of £2,500 to build a council flat in St Pancras in 1960. This was financed with loans repayable over sixty years, bringing the total cost to £8,200. In other words most rent was paid not to cover the costs of building but provided a safe bet for banks.

An analysis by the *Manchester Guardian* newspaper confirmed that spiralling land prices and hefty commercial interest rates were at the root of the deficit problem in St Pancras. Without subsidies from central government the council was forced to finance its housing programme by borrowing on the open market. As a consequence, the paper calculated that for every £100 that St Pancras collected in rent, £51 went on paying interest charges, £15 on debt repayments, £22 on repairs and £12 was spent on management. Without central government subsidies it looked as though St Pancras ratepayers would be in for some very steep increases to pay for the housing but John Lawrence had an answer, one given by many a local authority leader over the years, about how the policy would be financed. At the next election, he said soothingly, 'We can reasonably expect a change of Government and a decent housing policy.'

The Credit Crunch

While waiting for financial salvation from a future Labour government, however, the immediate conditions became increasingly hostile for two reasons. First, the Conservative government gave companies what was, in effect, a corporate tax cut. In 1955 a new law reduced the rates of commercial premises by 20 per cent. This inevitably hit inner-city areas hard, like that of central London, because they had a high proportion of commercial premises. In St Pancras, the loss of revenue was estimated to be around £372,000 a year and was a bitter pill to swallow. 'It comes at a time when we are being driven crazy trying to find enough money to carry on with the social services to the borough,' said John Lawrence, 'And it gives a bonus to the largest and most prosperous section of the community.' The council leader predicted that 'there will have to be wholesale abandoning of our social services if we are to make up this tremendous loss ... This Bill is a complete blow to local Government's resources'. The local Tory leader, Tim Donovan, who had complained about the subsidy to council tenants, was now £50 a year better off from the revaluation of *his* business premises for example.

Worse followed later in the year, when interest rates rose steeply. The Tory stewardship of the post-war economy was characterised by what were known as 'stop-go' policies. In the late 1950s the Chancellor of the Exchequer tried to dampen down the economy, which was displaying perilously inflationary tendencies. The consumer boom, on which much of the Conservatives' popularity rested, needed to be curtailed but in raising interest rates the Chancellor hit all borrowers – including local authority house-building schemes. After the cuts in housing, subsidies from central government, local authorities like St Pancras were forced to increase their borrowing on the open market to finance housing development. John Lawrence was bitter about the rise in interest charges and, mocking Macmillan, he complained that 'the moneylenders have never had it so good … they've just topped another £12,000 from this council'. It was not just local authorities feeling the pinch, spiralling interest rates also wrecked other local housing schemes too. The St Pancras Housing Association, led by anti-apartheid campaigner Father Trevor Huddleston, described 1956 as 'an infuriating and frustrating year' because of the credit squeeze which forced them to curtail building schemes. They described the latest rise as a 'deadly blow' to their plans for hundreds of new flats to replace slums in the area.

The District Auditor Moves In

The legal watchdog with the power to ensure that local authority spending was properly accounted for and remained within the law was called the district auditor. The district auditor can surcharge – effectively fine – individual councillors if they vote to spend rate revenue in ways which they are not legally allowed to do and in the late 1950s he was keeping an especially close eye on the policies of St Pancras Council.

Councillors were repeatedly warned by town hall officials that the housing policy might involve unwarrantable levels of spending, indebtedness and/or become an excessive burden for ratepayers. When rents were first lowered, officials issued a formal warning to councillors, who were obliged to record that 'we have borne in mind the comments of the chief officers of the council who have reported to us very fully on the implications of the scheme'. But they went ahead anyway, because 'we consider that rents of the housing accommodation should be within the reach of the majority of the council's prospective tenants and with this in mind, we consider that these rents are reasonable'.

In the summer of 1957, the district auditor arrived in St Pancras to open the annual audit and expressed his disquiet. Peggy Duff recalled that:

> [It] was the first time we were in trouble with the District Auditor. But we were lucky. I was able to persuade the District Auditor that ... it had become more difficult to let the higher flats, that tenants had to be transferred to fill them, and that too few tenants or tenants-to-be were willing to pay extra for the privilege of a view.

At this point, the district auditor was no more enthusiastic about getting involved with local political arguments over rents than he was with civil defence (*see* Chapter 4). Although petitioned by people complaining about the council's spending, he said that he was 'loath to interfere' with the rent levels and that by and large the policy of this council is not unreasonable'. But he did extract a promise from the councillors to keep the rents under constant review. With surging rents in the private sector it was not difficult to understand what that meant.

The Requisitioned Tenants

At first sight, the relatively small group of people in the requisitioned houses appeared to be what one councillor described as 'a minor issue'. However unwittingly, they were now about to pull together various strands of housing policy and present the councillors in St Pancras with a major challenge. The tenants in the requisitioned houses paid their rent to the council which, in turn, paid the owners for the use of the properties. The 1957 Rent Act had allowed the owners to demand higher market rents for these houses. An alarming gap began to open up between the controlled rent charged by the council and rent levels being set by the market. St Pancras Council made up the difference by subsidising the tenants in requisitioned properties from the general rate fund.

The councillors felt that they had a moral obligation to treat these tenants as their own and 'since the council has not imposed any rent increases on its own tenants we feel that there is no justification in imposing rent increases on these tenants'. Moreover, much of the requisitioned property had not been properly maintained since before the war and was now seriously dilapidated. As one council report put it, 'Most of this requisitioned property is in poor condition condition ... which has arisen as a result of the council's inability to spend money on proper repairs. The council has, in some cases, carried out improvements but these are only emergency measures and the properties have therefore deteriorated over the years.' Peggy Duff went so far as to claim that architects inspecting some requisitioned property had to be accompanied by male shorthand writers rather than the usual female stenographers who would have been too queasy about the conditions they witnessed.

As a consequence of the neglect, the council claimed that the requisitioned properties were now part of a Dickensian netherworld inhabited by 'special families and ... poorer families who could not afford the rents of the council's permanent estates; it appears therefore that a particularly unfortunate section of the population is living in these properties and we do not feel justified in agreeing to rent increases being imposed on these people'.

All this was apparently legal if the council could justify the subsidy in each individual case. But in no single case did the council pass the increase onto the tenant and Peggy Duff later confessed that 'the Town Clerk warned us that if we refused to pass on the increases, en bloc, we were in for trouble. Each case must be examined on its merits. This we did.' Or at least in theory, because despite endless forms and interviews, the councillors never passed on any increases to the occupants. Even Peggy Duff lamented, 'If we had exempted only half a dozen we might have avoided surcharge.' But the exemptions were not made and surcharge was the next step.

'Trouble ... Glorious Trouble'

By 1958 the council was in an intractable position: the existing housing policy was heading towards the rocks and the councillors knew it. The deficit on the housing budget was about to reach £250,000 – an astronomical sum. It could be reduced by raising rents but this would hit the poorest and increase inequality. On the other hand, the building programme could be cut back but this would increase waiting lists without solving the immediate problem. Had council leaders taken the district auditor's advice to keep rents under constant review, the crisis might have been avoided, but they had not. As Peggy Duff reflected, 'We had proceeded on our way refusing, in spite of pressure from the Tories and the Labour right, to increase rents.' This turned out to be a critical mistake.

When the district auditor returned in the summer of 1958 for the annual vetting of the council's books he was again met with complaints about the cost of the housing policy by a group of ratepayers (or 'Tories in disguise' as Duff called them). He warned the council that the deficit needed to be reined in quickly and added a reminder about how the context of housing in central London had changed. The 1957 Rent Act had now provided 'a universal yardstick', he warned, 'which was an important factor and one which was likely to have important repercussions for all council tenants'. In terms far stronger than those used on his previous visit, the district auditor urged that a 'general review' of council rents was long overdue – in other words, the time had come for increases.

The pressure to raise rents could not have come at a worse time because the summer and autumn of 1958 were turbulent times for Labour in St Pancras. Council Leader John Lawrence and other leading councillors were expelled from the Labour Party and the entire local party was suspended. Labour still controlled the council – just – with the expelled councillors now sitting as independent socialists (*see* Chapter 6). The council was in conflict with the law for its policies on housing and civil defence. To avoid surcharging or worse, some humiliating policy U-turns would be needed. Rumours flew and in late 1958 a local press headline 'Labour Group Keep Right – civil defence and rents policy may go' was more of an odds-on certainty than a vague prediction.

In council meetings the Conservatives called for U-turns on housing policy and civil defence. Their position was clear: the Tories were in favour of raising rents and resuming civil defence. The Independent Socialists (as they now called themselves), led by Lawrence, were equally resolved to oppose either the resumption of civil defence or rent rises – whatever the consequences. Lawrence, as always, was ready for the barricades and told the meeting, 'Let us unite ourselves with the people of St Pancras to stop this terrorisation ... ignore their threats, take no notice, vote against them right down the line and we shall be in trouble but it will be glorious trouble against the whole Tory Government and their right to interfere with a local council.'

But by now Lawrence's rhetorical dust had lost its magic. Members of the Labour group struggled with the reality of being locked into a conflict with the district auditor, the government and the law which it would be impossible to win. A humiliating climbdown was inevitable and it came late in 1958 when Labour agreed to start reviewing – raising – rents in the new year. The review was carried out on the most benign terms possible and while there were increases they were nothing like those faced by tenants in the private sector under the 1957 Rent Act. And they were far less than the Tories wanted.

The general review of rents was a U-turn that put council policy back within the law, but the district auditor still had questions about requisitioned tenants. He decided that the councillors had ignored his warnings. When the owners of requisitioned properties demanded higher rents – as the law now entitled them to do – councillors had failed to pass on the increases to the tenants and instead paid the increases from the general housing budget. This the council was not entitled to do. The district auditor decided to surcharge councillors for the amount of requisitioned tenants' rent increases. In other words, councillors would have to pay this money from their own pockets.

That these were very serious consequences of these legal proceedings was evident to all. Individual councillors would be crippled by the payments, possibly bankrupted and probably debarred from office. They were given time to prepare a case and explain why they should not be surcharged. When the district auditor opened the hearing into the twenty-three councillors who had voted for the subsidy to requisitioned tenants, the public galleries of the town hall were packed and police held crowds at bay outside. Inside the council chamber, where the hearings took place, Labour councillors were represented by former Labour MP and barrister Ashley Bramall, while John Lawrence spoke for the Independent Socialists.

Bramall argued that the 1957 Rent Act standards did not apply to requisitioned tenants who were protected by the licences issued under the original wartime Act. He concluded that it was a case where there was a dual responsibility to ratepayer and tenant. John Lawrence agreed and said that the council had simply tried to treat their own tenants and the requisitioned tenants without any distinction; 'They are not just tenants in private houses ... The Government put them in a special class and the council was entitled to treat them as a special class.' He also dismissed a means test to find out if they could afford the increase because 'that was abhorrent to the council and anyway we didn't treat our own tenants like that'. Lawrence concluded that the district auditor's intervention was a political attack instigated by local Tories who 'hope by this means to overcome our whole rent policy. This is a purely political issue the objectors have raised. Whatever you decide it won't make the slightest difference to their rates.'

The district auditor listened carefully to these arguments and rejected them. The twenty-three councillors were surcharged for several hundreds of pounds, which few of them could afford to pay. They appealed to the High Court which, after much legal wrangling, decided that no councillors should be disbarred from office – as they might have been – but the surcharge remained so that councillors were left to lick their wounds and pay up. Peggy Duff reflected the sentiments of many of them when she commented ruefully, 'Some of us would have preferred it the other way round.'

The District Auditor put a painful full stop to Labour's bold, brave attempt to develop a radical housing policy in St Pancras. Like those in other parts of London, Labour councillors were angry and frustrated that their plans to develop a capital for the people were thwarted by a government which had other priorities. And, like other parts of London, the story might have ended there but in St Pancras it did not. Splits in the local Labour Party and the problems of housing were issues far from resolved.

Chapter 6

THE MERE MENTION OF ST PANCRAS

'Rents Up, Red Flag Down, Labour Out'
> Local newspaper headline the day after
> Labour lost the elections in St Pancras, May 1958.

One summer evening in 1958, Aneurin Bevan slammed down a valuable Sheraton chair during a monumental row with his disciple and future Labour leader Michael Foot. The solid chair survived the shock little better than their relationship, which was being shaken to the core. They were arguing about St Pancras with Bevan repeatedly bellowing 'You c*nt! You c*nt!' at Foot as the quarrel spiralled out of control. Relationships throughout the Labour Party were strained; not for the first time (or the last) Labour's policy on defence opened up bitter divisions at all levels in the party (*see* chapter 4). This spilled over into other unresolved differences so that colleagues, comrades and old friends like Foot and Bevan found themselves at odds over what Labour really stood for and the direction of travel.

In his otherwise hagiographic biography of Bevan, Foot recalled miserably how St Pancras became part of the toxic mix that divided them and others in the Labour Party during the late 1950s:

I recall one terrible evening in July when I met him [Bevan] and Jennie [Bevan's wife] accidentally at the Polish Embassy and they both returned to our house to drink a few reconciling nightcaps. Delicately for a few minutes we tiptoed round the explosive issue of the bomb only to stumble into some other too sensitive territory connected with one of the periodic campaigns of expulsion from the Party which the Organisational sub-committee of the National Executive was then engaged in on a near-Stalinite scale. Who was the aggressor in the argument, I cannot recall. Either I suggested that he had not done enough to stop the expulsion of a well-known St Pancras rebel, John Lawrence, or he made some too sweeping allegation against the protesters at his public meetings. Perhaps it was the mere mention of St Pancras which started it.

In St Pancras itself, fall-out over recent events in the borough was even more bitter. The policy on rents and civil defence had brought councillors into conflict with the law, surcharge and personal bankruptcy. The Red Flag debacle had ended in a farce which left councillors looking more like hooligans than principled politicians. In short, rather than the mass support of the working class, Labour in St Pancras was attracting nationwide notoriety and ridicule. It was in this context of division and anger that another battle for St Pancras – this one within the Labour Party was fought out in the spring and summer of 1958. This was important because it created the context for the rent strikes which were to follow. The explosion of violence over housing (*see* chapter 7) cannot be properly explained or understood without grasping the political culture that evolved in the years leading up to the riots.

In June 1958 the grandees of Labour's National Executive Committee (NEC), met at Transport House, the party's imposing headquarters in Smith Square opposite the Palace of Westminster. The NEC was responsible for party discipline and the situation in the Holborn and St Pancras South Labour Party was high up on the agenda for discussion. St Pancras Council had by now ceased to be just another Labour-controlled local authority managing vital services such as drains and libraries. It had become the most talked-about council in the country – and for all the wrong reasons as far as the NEC was concerned.

The National Executive could not, of course, interfere directly with the policies of a democratically elected council. But they could take control of a local Labour Party and the NEC now decided to call time on Holborn and St Pancras. The meeting opted to expel some thirty activists immediately – including fourteen councillors and John Lawrence – while the rest of the CLP was suspended until further notice. The power to suspend or expel party members was enshrined in the Labour Party rule book and as one party official commented during the process, 'I don't think that we have suspended an entire CLP before'. He was right, they hadn't. Michael Foot's hyperbolic accusation of 'Stalinist' was simply not true. As one Labour historian wrote later, 'Critics of Transport House sometimes gave the impression that apparatchiks from Head Office (in the 1950s) were let loose upon a constituency party running amok with machetes, and lopping off the heads of anyone who could be suspected of having disloyal thoughts. This was quite wrong.' What happened in St Pancras was the exception rather than the norm. And as so often, the events which unfolded in this local party were avidly covered by the national media.

Woodrow Wyatt and Witch Hunts

Early in 1958, a row blew up about the suspension of one local party member in Holborn and St Pancras. It did not involve John Lawrence or anyone on the left but Woodrow Wyatt, whose views were on the right of the party. Wyatt, who had been a Labour MP between 1945 and 1955, was on the list of approved parliamentary candidates and looking for another seat. He was originally a Bevanite, something that ought to have appealed to a left-wing party like Holborn and St Pancras, but he was not popular. Frequently aloof and patronising to others, he was thin-skinned and quick to take offence himself. Worse still, as far

Above: Holborn 1949, note the bomb site on the left. (© Copyright Ben Brooksbank and licensed for reuse under Creative Commons Licence)

Below: Building the New Jerusalem after the war with a new housing estate in Theobalds Road, Holborn. (© Copyright Ben Brooksbank and licensed for reuse under Creative Commons Licence)

Above and below: The office boom in the City of London after the Blitz led to soaring land prices in neighbouring boroughs like Holborn and St Pancras. The above photograph was taken in 1962 and the one below in 1955. (Both images © Copyright Ben Brooksbank and licensed for reuse under Creative Commons Licence)

Above and below: Two photographs showing the building of the new Barbican complex on the western edge of the city near St Pancras. (Both images © Copyright Ben Brooksbank and licensed for reuse under Creative Commons Licence)

Above: The attraction of the romantic steam age was lost on the residents of St Pancras who had to live with the pollution caused by three main railway stations in the district. The photograph shows trains at King's Cross in the 1950s. (© Copyright Ben Brooksbank and licensed for reuse under Creative Commons Licence)

Below: A train arriving at St Pancras station in the 1950s, complete with gas holders. (© Copyright Ben Brooksbank and licensed for reuse under Creative Commons Licence)

Above: St Pancras station in the 1950s. British Rail was a mainstay of the local economy. (© Copyright Ben Brooksbank and licensed for reuse under Creative Commons Licence)

Below: The Hampstead Garden suburb of Erskine Hill (seen here in the 1950s). Home ownership was an option for those who wanted to escape the smog and pollution of central London. (© Copyright Ben Brooksbank and licensed for reuse under Creative Commons Licence)

Above: Great Ormond Street, Holborn, in the 1950s. (© Copyright Ben Brooksbank and licensed for reuse under Creative Commons Licence)

Below: The Euston Road development made a fortune for property speculators but was a less beneficial project for people who actually lived in the area. (© Copyright Ben Brooksbank and licensed for reuse under Creative Commons Licence)

Above: Royal College Street in the centre of St Pancras, 1960. (© Copyright Ben Brooksbank and licensed for reuse under Creative Commons Licence)

Below: Chalk Farm and Gloucester Avenue in St Pancras, 1960. (© Copyright Ben Brooksbank and licensed for reuse under Creative Commons Licence)

Above: St Pancras Road, seen here in 1962, looks peaceful enough. But when police cordons blocked the way to the town hall at the bottom of the road, the rioting began in September 1960. The station is on the left. (© Copyright Ben Brooksbank and licensed for reuse under Creative Commons Licence)

Below left: When Don Cook was evicted from his flat in this block in Leighton Road, NW5, in September 1960 it triggered the St Pancras rent riots. (© Copyright Mike Quinn and licensed for reuse under Creative Commons Licence)

Below right: Ken Loach's harrowing film *Cathy Come Home* raised Britain's housing crisis up the political agenda. But for many it was too late. (Garnett and Loach)

as many activists in Holborn and St Pancras were concerned, he was moving rapidly towards the right wing of the Labour Party. In the autumn of 1957, he used his position as a journalist on the BBC's *Panorama* programme to make a hard-hitting report into the take-over of the Electrical Trades Union (ETU) by communists alleging, among other things, that they had rigged ballots. A ferocious battle for control of the union ensued and the case became a cause célèbre. In his memoirs Frank Chapple, leader of the non-communist faction in the ETU, described Wyatt as 'our best media friend' at this time but it made him plenty of enemies in the Holborn and St Pancras Labour Party where he was a member. (Wyatt's intellectual journey to the right continued, as did his obsession with communism. He subsequently became a media cheerleader for Thatcherism and is probably best known now as the father of columnist Petronella Wyatt.)

The local party narrowly passed a resolution demanding that Wyatt's name be removed from the list of approved candidates because of his 'anti-working class activities and witch-hunting good trade unionists'.

The demand was predictably rejected by party bosses, who were by now looking to remove not Wyatt but activists of the Holborn and St Pancras Labour Party from membership lists. Labour officials investigating the Holborn and St Pancras General Management Committee (GMC) – the main forum for decision making in a constituency Labour Party – found that more than a score of delegates did not live in the borough and so were not eligible to sit on the committee. The local press ran the news as a front page lead under the headline 'Labour Party Bid to Break Red Domination – 21 Delegates Turned Off Committee' and commented, 'This mass expulsion follows a move by the London Labour Party to break the communist domination of the area organisation.' More changes followed swiftly. In March 1958 members of the hard left Lawrence faction were defeated in elections for party posts. Two refugees from Nazi Germany were among those who took now took charge. George and

Irene Wagner had both developed a profound antipathy to the revolutionary left; they thought that the communists' failure to support the Weimar constitution had played a part in allowing Hitler to grab power in 1933 and communism now had an iron grip on a substantial chunk of their homeland. The need to fight within the existing democratic political framework had been seared into the Wagners' political psyche, and both distrusted John Lawrence who they believed would fail in his revolutionary aspirations and merely alienate other progressive people from the Labour Party. They also believed the increasingly restive presence of Oswald Mosley's Union Movement was attracted to St Pancras in reaction to Lawrence.

For the next two months competing factions wrestled for control of the Holborn and St Pancras Labour Party. Then, when the Red Flag celebrations of 1 May descended into chaos it was, for many members, the final straw: they wanted Lawrence out. When the GMC convened on 15 May, the agenda was dominated by a resolution from Holborn, which read: 'In view of the activities of John Lawrence which continue to discredit the Labour Party this GMC ... resolves to expel him from membership.' The short resolution triggered a long splenetic debate that lasted three hours, during which members traded insults and almost came to blows. The vote, when it came, could scarcely have been closer and the resolution was lost by just two votes: 31 – 33.

Outside, the press pack waited like a flock of vultures to pick over Labour's embarrassment. The *Daily Mail* reported that when the meeting broke up, 'Red Flag Lawrence [as the paper now called him] stood exultantly in the rain ... after a move to throw him out of the Labour Party had been defeated. His "Keep Left" supporters kept him in the party.' But Lawrence's exultation was brief. Those opposed to the council Leader gathered in the Wagners' Bloomsbury flat that night and planned an appeal to the NEC. They penned a litany of complaints about the 'organised group' which they claimed had taken control of the local party and listed specific allegations, including charges of intimidation, the misuse of party funds, and establishment of links with other groups such as the Communist Party. The letter concluded:

> For several years the rest of the party (which has, after all, a long radical tradition) has accepted many things unwillingly in order to preserve unity; discussion of issues on their merits has become almost impossible. We hoped that a change might be brought about by normal means. We have now regretfully decided that this is unlikely, and that the present state of affairs can be tolerated no longer. We can assure you that there will be a substantial body of opinion inside the party ready to support any action the National Executive Committee may decide to take to improve matters.

In fact, Labour's chiefs needed little prompting to take action. Minutes show that the NEC was on the case and that they had already embarked on an investigation of the Holborn and St Pancras South party. The powerful NEC chairmen's subcommittee had held a special meeting early in March 1958 at the House of Commons. The main agenda item was how to deal with the ultra-left Victory For Socialism; the group was alleged to be organising a 'party within a party', which was strictly against the Labour Party rules. Minutes of this meeting reveal that the party's omnipresent General Secretary, Morgan Phillips, also reported 'difficulties' in the St Pancras Labour Group. The subcommittee resolved to order an inquiry which was swiftly carried out.

As a result of this investigation the NEC decided that Lawrence should be 'suspended from membership and asked if he could show cause why he should not be expelled'. Perhaps the presence of left-wingers including Aneurin Bevan, Barbara Castle, Ian Nikardo and Tom Driberg (who chaired the NEC) helped

Lawrence avoid immediate expulsion. Morgan Phillips then wrote to Lawrence telling him about the NEC's verdict:

> The National Executive Committee has been giving consideration to your general activities and views, which appear to be inimical to the best interests of the Labour Party and indistinguishable from known communists. It has therefore decided to suspend you from Labour Party membership forthwith, and to give you an opportunity of making such representations as you think desirable before it considers the further steps to be taken.

Lawrence's suspension immediately hit the national news – *The Times* said it was part of a move to root out 'a vigorous group of ex-Trotskyists active in the constituency'. Morgan Phillips tried to avoid getting into details and told journalists that it was down to an 'accumulation of happenings'. For his part, Lawrence feigned bewilderment and told the press, 'I do not yet know why I have been suspended. I have a fair idea though; they don't like my politics.' That much was certainly true. But what were the parts of John Lawrence's politics that Labour didn't like? Oddly, Phillips' letter did not contain any specific charges – there was no attempt to single out one speech or policy which so departed from Labour orthodoxy that it called for his expulsion.

Believe What You Want – Labour's Confusion

As his letter had not contained any specific charges, Lawrence phoned Phillips to find out which particular activities or views had led to his suspension. The call led to exchanges which at times bordered on the surreal. Labour in the 1950s was frequently described as 'a broad church' with competing visions. The party's constitution of 1918 laid down the means by which it would seek power – parliamentary democracy – but what it would do with power remained an open question. Various groups within the party (like the Bevanites) or intellectual politicians (like Tony Crosland) had tried to come up with coherent ideas of Labour's purpose but this seemed to trigger off more faction fighting rather than lead to a definitive answer (*see* chapter 2).

In the summer of 1958, this confusion presented the NEC with something of a problem when attempting to sanction John Lawrence. What, exactly, had he said that others in the party were not saying or actually done that was against party rules? It was far from clear. So instead of levelling detailed charges against Lawrence, the NEC delved into history and Lawrence's associates. Morgan Phillips reminded Lawrence of his past memberships of the Revolutionary Communist Party, the Socialist Fellowship movement and his editorship of the magazine *Socialist Outlook*. And to bring the story up to date, Phillips cited Lawrence's actual involvement with the Holborn and St Pancras United Workers and Tenants Defence Committee, (UWTDC), 'in which Communists play an active part'. The letter also complained that Lawrence had spoken less than a month before, and at the outset of the London County Council election campaign, on a platform alongside the Communist Party candidate Jock Nicholson. Phillips concluded:

> During recent years and months, your public declarations reveal you have very little in common with democratic socialism, so much so that when asked if you intended to rejoin the Communist Party, your answer was 'why should I want to leave a big Party to join a small one. I want to get things done.' There is no hint of any difference of opinion with the Communist Party: indeed, on a subsequent occasion, you made it clear that 'there is not much difference between socialism and communism'. Other instances of the declarations of your views could be given if necessary, but I think I have said sufficient to amplify the point made in my original letter that they do appear to be inimical to the best interests of the Labour Party.

Lawrence sent a lengthy reply to the NEC. He rebutted both the allegations about his past and current views and threw in some pertinent questions of his own. Lawrence cited Nye Bevan who had said something similar about China:

> He [Bevan] said, at a public meeting, that were he Chinese he would be in the Chinese Communist Party for the same reason that, being British, he is in the Labour Party – because both these parties are mass parties of the workers and could get things done. It would seem that if Mr Bevan would work for communism in China or socialism in Britain, he doesn't think there is a lot of difference between them.

Incidentally, adulation of Red China did not stop then. Even in the 1990s Labour MP Tony Benn described Chairman Mao as 'the greatest man of the 20th century'.

Lawrence was also puzzled about information which the party had known for years. 'Why now does (my past) become grounds for suspension and possible expulsion?' His past was well known and there were, he pointed out, plenty of other ex-communists in the Labour Party. 'Dragging in my past membership of Socialist Fellowship and editorship of *Socialist Outlook* is also irrelevant. Why now, after all these years, do these things become a reason for suspension? And why is it only applied to me? The Socialist Fellowship had thousands of members – including a lot of MPs.' These were indeed very pertinent questions.

Lawrence concluded that the real reason for his expulsion was because he had led a council that 'earned itself a reputation for defying the Tory Government and for refusing to meekly acquiesce in Tory policy'. He then listed some of the council's policies and quoted a few of the press headlines that had gleefully greeted his suspension and concluded:

> The press has at least judged us on what we have done. They know, as you know, that I do not write books or produce a regular column in the Sunday newspapers. My views must, therefore, be

expressed through my political activities. You have omitted all reference to these activities and that, in my opinion, is the most significant thing in the whole of [your] lengthy letter.

Lawrence had a point. If his political past was a cause for concern – which it legitimately was – more searching questions surely should have been asked of him before he was allowed to join the Labour Party in the late 1940s. The party had debarred him from being a parliamentary candidate in 1954 even though he would have stood against Churchill and been bound to lose. Yet he was allowed to become the leader of a London council with real powers just two years later. In reality it was not his past but his current actions on St Pancras Council which led to his suspension, but none of these were ever clearly identified by Morgan Phillips. It could have been shown that whereas politicians on the left like Nye Bevan held a core belief in parliamentary democracy and constitutional law, John Lawrence did not. Lawrence had demonstrated time and again that almost any means – from extra parliamentary mass action the illegal use of council powers – were legitimate if they accelerated the advance towards a workers' state. It was a crucial dividing line but to a large extent the real reasons for his expulsion – the effect of St Pancras' policies on the image of the Labour Party nationally – were never discussed. The truth was that Labour just wanted Lawrence out of the way and the embarrassments stemming from St Pancras Council to cease as fast as possible.

Lawrence's political failing was that he was out of kilter with the time and tide of the Labour Party. Timing is vital in politics, and Lawrence's was out. Nye Bevan was moving to the centre. Whatever Bevan's admiration for Chinese communism may or may not have been, in Britain he was utterly committed to winning power through democratic channels (which was not an option in China). The same cannot be said of John Lawrence, who repeatedly demonstrated that he thought mass working-class movements could lead to a socialist administration, by whatever route. Bevan was now rediscovering the pragmatism which had made him such a remarkably successful minister in government. He was engineering a rapprochement with the Gaitskellite wing of the Labour Party – prepared even to alienate his erstwhile supporters – and was more concerned with cohesive leadership than on staking out positions within the party. Bevan understood the need for unity where Lawrence did not, and was prepared to make the necessary compromises that Lawrence detested as 'cant, humbug and hypocrisy'.

Lawrence then defended himself against the charge of close associations with the communists in St Pancras through various tenants' organisations. He did not deny that communists were active in these organisations but argued that communists were active in the Trade Union movement too. 'It is something to their credit,' wrote Lawrence.

> The tenant organisations referred to are bodies which exist to defend tenants against landlords and their friends the Tory Government. They are not political organisations and, as yet, they are not proscribed (by the Labour Party). They are, in fact, rather primitive organisations, which allow tenants of all political persuasions to unite their efforts against a common enemy. When such organisations hold demonstrations against the Rent Act, as we did in the meeting at which the communist, Mr Nicholson, was one of the speakers, the only condition for participation is a readiness to resist the impositions placed on tenants by the Tory Government. To infer that Labour Party members should boycott such organisations simply because communists are active in them is cold war socialism in all its nakedness.

Lawrence's defence of his involvement in the UWTDC revealed again the problem of communist 'front' organisations which had bedevilled the Labour Party to a much larger extent before the war and earlier in the 1950s. At a national level the NEC could, and did, proscribe them (i.e. make their membership incompatible with membership of the Labour Party) but contact with communists in any number of organisations like the UWTDC was inevitable. Lawrence's defence of his association with other groups on the left might have been rather more convincing, however, had he not simultaneously been instrumental in a bid to remove Woodrow Wyatt's name from Labour's list of candidates. Lawrence was relaxed about appearing with a candidate from another party during an election campaign whist condemning a fellow member of his own party. Wyatt's 'crime' was not that he supported the 1957 Rent Act – which he certainly did not – but that he had openly criticised the methods of communists in the ETU. Lawrence obviously thought that Labour had no enemies on the left but that social democrats were another matter.

Labour's move against Lawrence revealed that far from being the 'Stalinist' organisation conjured up by Michael Foot, the party organisation was actually rather hesitant and uncertain of itself. If there was a charge of Stalinism to be made it might have been better levelled at John Lawrence. He had fallen out with his erstwhile Trotskyist comrades because of an increasing sympathy with the USSR and in an interview with the *Sunday Times* in April 1957 he had boasted that 'Russia is the number one country today'. He went on to explain that he was in favour of the abolition of private property and wanted a classless society. As for St Pancras Council, 'We were elected to do socialist things. We intend to use the council to inspire in ordinary people the hatred and contempt for capitalist society which we feel ourselves ... I think, with Marx, that you need a revolution to get rid of the privileged classes and the muck of ages in men's minds.'

Lawrence tried to explain away some of the complaints made about him and his caucus by other members of the party to the NEC. He defended the deselection of some councillors in 1956 as 'just part of the normal democratic process which allowed activists to express their views'. The rowdy party meetings were because 'noisy interruptions (on all sides) are, I'm afraid to say, a feature of many public meetings ... how this constitutes "intimidation" is beyond me.' The holding of open votes rather than secret ballots? Lawrence argued that 'There can be differences about that – but they hardly call for the wholesale "reorganisation" of the Party.' 'The allegation that donations had been made to "doubtful causes"? All donations from the party were agreed by a majority vote' and so on.

Finally, Lawrence argued that recent electoral success in the LCC elections in the spring of 1958 were an endorsement of his strategy on the council. 'It is then alleged that my activities have prevented the effective political and electoral functioning of the Party. Facts speak for themselves. In Holborn and St Pancras South we recently gained, for the first time, all three seats on the London County Council.' As Napoleon said of war, 'a victory has many parents but defeat is an orphan' and the same is true of elections. In fact, Labour was returned to County Hall with a landslide victory across the whole of London. It would have been a spectacular mishap had the party not swept up Holborn and St Pancras too. The result was less an endorsement of Lawrence's leadership than a mid-term protest against the government in the aftermath of Suez; as eminent psephologist David Butler commented, 'After the Second World War the results of local government elections became increasingly accepted as barometers of the national political mood.' In any case the NEC was unmoved by Lawrence's arguments and confirmed its decision to expel Lawrence from the Labour Party.

St Pancras Splits

The expulsion created an immediate headache for the Labour group on the council. In May, Lawrence had been officially confirmed as both leader of the Labour group and leader of the council for the following year. He was now the leader of a party group to which he did not belong and leader of a council where he was the sole independent councillor. Nevertheless, other councillors were quick to rally to his support and the Labour group went into emergency session to decide how to deal with the problem. A resolution asking the NEC to meet with the Labour group – which had not been consulted at any stage about the suspension of their Leader – was carried unanimously. But it did nothing to decide the key question: did councillors stand by Lawrence or were they going to remain members of the Labour Party and let him swing in the wind?

The group convened again to discuss a resolution to reaffirm Lawrence as their leader. It was effectively a vote of confidence – and it was lost. Fourteen councillors voted to support Lawrence and when the result was announced they walked out of the meeting. The fourteen issued a defiant statement saying that they intended to fight the decision to suspend Lawrence from within the party. 'This is not a battle over one man or one man's policies – it is a battle over what kind of policies the Labour Party shall have,' they insisted. On that much, at least, all sides could agree. At the end of May 1958, the existing Labour group met for the last time. The stormy meeting lasted for some three and a half hours and the main point at issue was whether they could continue to be led by a man who was no longer a member of the Labour Party. The majority, 19–15, decided that it could not. The fifteen walked out while those remaining looked at one another, dazed by the flurry of events. Those who had decided to split from Labour announced that they were now the St Pancras Socialist Labour Group and they were, said Lawrence, 'at war with the National Executive Committee of the Labour Party'.

The new leadership were reluctant to surrender either the moral high ground of socialist values or even the socialist epithet to the breakaway group. They also wanted to make it quite clear that there would be no change of direction or policy by the new regime, which they would continue to fight for socialism within the party and on the council.

> We wish to emphasise, therefore, that the policies of the St Pancras Borough Council over the last two years have been the policies of the Labour Group, and not just the leader, and that the reason given for his expulsion by the NEC did not include any of these policies. There has been no investigation of the Labour Group or its policies, and no criticism by the NEC.

The claim that there had been no criticism of the council's policies by the NEC was, at the very least, a sleight of hand. The real reasons for Lawrence's expulsion were precisely because of the policies pursued by the council with him at the helm. But because the charges against Lawrence had never been specified in detail, the councillors could get away with the fiction.

While the Labour group on the council was thrown into turmoil by Lawrence's expulsion, the Holborn and St Pancras South Labour Party was being completely reorganised. The CLP officers supplied a list of members who were firmly identified with Lawrence. Those not on the list were invited back into the party, but only after they had signed a declaration that they were on the electoral role, not members of a proscribed organisation, and that they would conform to the 'constitution, programme and principles' of the CLP. There were grumbling resolutions about the abrupt methods used and a local affiliated union branch, the ever vociferous porters of the TGWU in Covent Garden market, were upset – the *Daily Telegraph* reported the 'Row in the Market'. But otherwise there was little complaint from ordinary party members and the process of reorganisation was actually remarkable for the lack of reaction rather than the reverse.

The whole reorganisation was conducted swiftly and according to natural justice. All the activists, including those most closely associated with the Lawrence caucus, were given ample opportunity to explain their views and express a belief in democratic socialism if they so wished. Others merely had to restate a belief in the 'principles, policy and programme' of the party (as contained in the Constitution) and agree to cooperate with the NEC (which was democratically elected by the whole party). The image of heavy-handed bureaucrats arbitrarily imposing their right-wing creed on a resistant CLP – as portrayed by John Lawrence and apologists like Michael Foot – was a fantasy.

Given the seismic nature of the shock that hit the Holborn and St Pancras party, the real surprise was just how few members were directly affected by the turbulence. The Lawrence caucus, which had dominated the left in the party, was actually very small if it is defined in terms of the members who were expelled from or left the party in the summer of 1958. Just thirty activists refused to cooperate with the NEC, and almost half of these were councillors. On the other side, the anti-Lawrence faction was organised by just four people and their strength lay in being able to attract rapid support from twenty-one other influential party activists (ward chairs, secretaries etc.). In 1956, the total CLP membership stood at 1,126 (711 men and 415 women) and although the anti-Lawrence faction complained of a decline in membership, it is unlikely to have dropped massively. If these figures even roughly reflect the accurate membership figures of 1958, it suggests that no more than 5 per cent of CLP members were actively associated with either faction. Most Labour Party members just did not want to get involved. Denis Healy once said that the difference between a dictatorship and a democracy is that in a dictatorship 1 in 100 people get involved in politics, and in a democracy it is 2 in 100. Perhaps the same has more truth for ordinary members too than many party leaders like to recognise.

'We Don't Intend to Drop Dead'

In a final bid to get reinstated, the Lawrence caucus now prepared to mobilise support for an appeal to the annual conference of the Labour Party. They began by appealing for popular support in St Pancras, leafleting parts of the borough and holding public meetings. By the end of August they claimed that around 5,000 people from Holborn and St Pancras had signed a petition supporting their readmission into the Labour Party.

If these figures were accurate, they might suggest that there was much support for the rebel councillors. But they might also be seen as a result of failure. Having failed to persuade the majority of Labour activists to back them, the Lawrence group was now appealing for support over the heads of party members. And this could mean almost anyone: there was no way of checking whether the signatories were Labour voters or others. Were some local Tories or even the Union Movement all gleefully out to further destabilise the local Labour Party among the signatories? Who knows. But, when this support was put to the harsh reality of an electoral test in the subsequent local elections, it collapsed. Lawrence and the other expelled councillors only won a tiny fraction of 5,000 votes.

Support did come from some other CLPs around the country: around fifty of over 600 CLPs sent resolutions of solidarity and a total of £140 was collected from donations. However, even these messages tended to confine themselves to criticising the form of the NEC action rather than express support for the politics of John Lawrence. Most called for Lawrence to be given a chance to put his case to Labour Party conference that autumn so that he could 'be given a fair hearing'. They did not presuppose a verdict.

In mid-July the NEC had ruled that there was no provision for such an appeal, although Lawrence argued that Sir Stafford Cripps had been allowed to appeal to conference after his expulsion from the Labour Party in 1939. And in the 1980s, expelled members of the Militant Tendency were given time to put their case to conference, so it might be thought that Lawrence was treated a little harshly. Delegates to the conference cannot have been unaware of the arguments though;

Lawrence compiled a well-produced twenty-page booklet outlining his version of events, which was distributed at the conference – the front cover featured a picture of the Red Flag flying over the town hall. On the afternoon of 30 September, Conference went into private session. The Conference Arrangements Committee reported that it had received a letter from Lawrence asking to be allowed to speak to Conference in his own defence. It had examined the Constitution and Standing Orders but was unable to find any provision for people or organisations expelled by the NEC to appeal to Conference. Peggy Duff, the delegate from St Pancras North Labour Party, moved the suspension of Standing Orders so that Lawrence could be heard. She was seconded by Frank Cousins, the enormously powerful General Secretary of the Transport and General Workers' Union. But according to Duff even his support had a caveat: he spoke up for Lawrence, said Duff, 'not because he had any particular interest in the case, but because he felt strongly that there ought to be some proper machinery for appeals against expulsion'. In any event, even with the support of the most powerful union in the country, the motion was defeated by 4,101,000 to 2,531,000. When Duff then forced a vote to strike out the section of the NEC report dealing with St Pancras it was crushed by a huge margin of 6,019,000 to 476,000. The vote was clear and the vast majority of the Labour movement agreed with what the NEC had done.

The defeat at the conference marked the end of John Lawrence's strange career in the Labour Party. It also put a full stop to any influence which his group hoped to retain within Labour. Before the conference decision Lawrence said that 'None of us intends to drop dead if the Labour Party refuse to take us back.' Nevertheless, the political afterlife beckoned. Many activists who had gone along with the policies of the council now faced an inescapable conflict of loyalty. When forced to choose between Lawrence and Labour, they chose Labour. Even many of the expelled councillors were discombobulated and confused about what to do next. Some wondered if it was worth continuing in politics at all.

They were soon forced to make a decision. A by-election was forced by the resignation of a councillor who stood down because of illness. By chance, the vacant seat was one of those in the Somers Town ward, which was represented by John Lawrence. The local press thought the by-election promised to be 'the most exciting ... for a vacancy in St Pancras Borough Council since the war', not least because the other councillors for the ward – all of whom had just been expelled from Labour – decided to back the Communist Party candidate, John Taylor. Taylor was a familiar, if unlikely, ally for the rebel group. He had left his public school to become a captain in the army during the war and, as the CP's central London organiser, was heavily involved in the St Pancras United Workers and Tenants Defence Committee. Lawrence and the other ward councillors worked tirelessly for Taylor. They knew the ward. They visited every Somers Town resident who had signed the petition against their expulsion from the Labour Party. They distributed leaflets calling for working-class unity between the Labour and Communist parties to defeat the Tories. The result was a humiliating defeat for the Communist Party. The Labour candidate, a local pipe-fitter, topped the poll. That was no surprise but Taylor lagged behind even the Tory candidate, a milkman and an active member of the TGWU.

After backing the Communist candidate in the election, and having now publicly admitted that CP policy on local government was identical to his own, Lawrence actually joined the CP in December 1958. He was joined by six other councillors and about a dozen of the expelled activists. But the centralised discipline of the Communist Party did not suit Lawrence. After six months he left, though whether this was of his choosing or the CP's was not clear. Leaving two political parties within a year did not deter him from remaining active in the borough and the events which were about to unfold. He was particularly active during the rent strike and was jailed for three months for his part in it. During the 1960s his interest in politics diminished, however, and he became increasingly less active. In old age he retained only a vestigial sympathy for any kind of socialism and was particularly scathing about the ideals and rhetoric of the Labour left in London.

Other leading members of the expelled group did not join Lawrence in the Communist Party but continued to sit as Independents on the council under the chairmanship of Jock Stallard. Stallard's reluctance to join the CP was perhaps the biggest surprise, and was apparently grounded in a newly discovered pragmatism. Stallard argued that there was no point in standing as either an Independent or as a CP candidate at the next election and that there was therefore no point in joining the CP; he hinted that he would try to rejoin the Labour Party, which he did in 1962 without much difficulty. It turned out to be a wise career move. Stallard became the MP for St Pancras North and ended up as a member of the House of Lords. Other councillors also thought that joining the CP was a mistake and continued to sit on the council as Independent Socialists until the election in May 1959 when they stood down. Alderman Charles Taylor said that he would sit out the remainder of his time as an Independent Socialist and, as events turned out, his was a crucial position during the rent strike two years later.

The infighting in the local party was an enormous distraction and left it ill prepared to fight elections. But despite the chaos, the results in 1958–59 were mixed, and the analysis of the results leads to some surprisingly counter-intuitive conclusions. Between April 1958 and October 1959 there were three elections in Holborn and St Pancras: for the London County Council, the Borough Council and Parliament. In the LCC elections of April 1958 the CLP selected three candidates who were firmly identified with John Lawrence. They included Tom Braddock, his ally from the *Socialist Outlook* magazine (*see* Chapter 2), and

Louis Bondy (*see* chapter 9). All three were returned in what was a marked London-wide swing to Labour and the local upheaval did not have any noticeable effect on the Labour vote.

The results were less good for the council elections of May 1959. Labour lost control of St Pancras Council, but this too was in line with the nationwide swing against Labour. Nationally, in the local elections held on the same day, Labour lost well over 200 seats and control of nineteen authorities. Although the St Pancras result was described as 'spectacular' and one of the most interesting of the night in the national press, the change of control was actually down to a tiny swing – around 100 votes – in one marginal ward which had been hotly contested between Labour and the Tories since the war. The biggest drubbing of the night was reserved for John Lawrence and his fellow Communist Party candidates. Despite fighting in the ward that he had represented for six years, turnout was low and his vote plummeted. Of the sixteen candidates in the ward, Lawrence came second to bottom. Every communist candidate was at least 1,100 votes behind any Labour candidate; they were all pushed into a derisory third place behind all the Tory candidates.

Having lost control of the council in the spring of 1959, the macro-political climate became measurably worse for Labour as the year wore on. The Tory Party was fast recovering from the poor premiership of Anthony Eden and Harold Macmillan had established himself as an able prime minister. 'Supermac', as he was dubbed, now inflated the economy and the Conservatives regained their confidence in the wake of the Suez debacle. At the general election of 1959, the Tories increased their majority to 100; one of the seats that changed hands was Holborn and St Pancras South. The Labour share of the poll nationally fell from 46.6 per cent to 43.3 per cent – a drop of 2.6 per cent. In Holborn and St Pancras South, Labour's share of the vote fell but by less than the national average. Despite the turmoil over the Lawrence expulsion, support for Labour in Holborn and St Pancras held up better than in any of the surrounding constituencies. The loss of the seat was most plausibly explained by the absence of a Liberal candidate, whose support appears to have swung to the moderate and well-known Conservative, Geoffrey Johnson-Smith (*see* chapter 9).

The loss of the council and the parliamentary seat were heavy blows for Labour. It might have been thought that leftist, radical politics would now have time in which to draw breath, recuperate and reflect in a period of quietude after the traumas of the past three years. These were logical considerations, but wholly erroneous. St Pancras was actually heading for a Force 10 political storm that would shake the nation.

Chapter 7

RENT STRIKES AND RIOTS

'Hundreds of police have just charged a crowd in the Euston Road and are locked face to face in the most vicious fighting I have yet seen. I heard dozens of women screaming as they went down ... Unconscious men, blood streaming from their faces, were dragged across the street.'

Daily Express journalist Clifford Luton, September 1960

Hey Ho! Cook and Rowe!
(or: *The Landlord's Nine Questions*)
As true a story I'll relate
(With a) HEY HO! COOK AND ROWE!
How the landlord told Don Cook one night,
(With a) HEY HO! COOK AND ROWE!
You must answer questions nine
(With a) HEY HO! COOK AND ROWE!
To see if your flat is yours or mine
(With a) HEY HO! COOK AND ROWE!
CHORUS:
Hey, ho, tell them no
With a barb-wire fence and a piano,
Took a thousand cops to make them go,
Three cheers for Cook and Rowe!
What is higher than a tree?

And what is lower than a flea?
My rent is higher than a tree,
And the landlord's lower than a flea.
(CHORUS)
What goes on and never stops?
And what is gentler than a cop?
The tenants' fight will never stop
And the devil is gentler than a cop.
(CHORUS)
What is stronger than a door?
And tell me what a roof is for?
Barb-wire is stronger, here's your proof,
The bailiffs came in through the roof.
(CHORUS)
Will you get off my property?
Or will you pay the rent to me?
We've settled in as you can see,
Now, won't you stop for a cup of tea?
(CHORUS)
O, now I've lost my board and bed,
I'll barricade the streets instead.
So all you tenants, settle in,
Keep up the fight, you're bound to win.
(CHORUS)
Song about the battle of St Pancras with music and words
by Peggy Seeger and Ewan MacColl

Deficit reduction was the Tories overriding priority when they won control of St Pancras town hall in May 1959. The Conservative government had cut back grants for council house-building programmes since the mid-1950s while a fever of speculation gripped the London property market, forcing the cost of land and building in the city ever higher. It was a fatal combination: decreasing grants and rising costs meant that the building programme in St Pancras was increasingly financed from the rates and the deficit ballooned (*see* Chapter 5). Labour had pegged rents at relatively low levels, which councillors believed tenants could afford, but this meant that income to the housing budget – known as the Housing Revenue Account (HRA) – was nowhere near enough to cover the increasing costs. It was estimated that the HRA deficit in 1959–60 would be just over £300,000 (around £6.5 million today). The Tories argued that without radical action the deficit would become wholly unsustainable. By today's standards these figures are small change in the London housing market and would scarcely cover the cost of one of the capital's smarter homes. At the time, however, they were astronomic and all sides agreed that something would have to be done about the spiralling deficit.

Homes and Rents: Who Pays?

The key questions were about who should pay for the costs of housing in central London. The tenants alone through their rents? Or should the cost be spread more widely across all the ratepayers in the borough? In the autumn of 1960, the *New Statesman* described the Conservative answer as 'the law of supply and demand must apply to housing as to ... TV sets. If you cannot afford a TV set you must go without it. If you cannot afford to live in London you must live somewhere else. But where?' It was a good question then, and one that many are asking again today. Labour insisted that housing was a social service with positive external benefits for the whole community. It was quite right then, that the whole community should contribute to replace lost government grants, not least because around 70 per cent of council income came from rates paid by businesses located in the borough (the biggest being British Rail). As Labour's housing spokesperson, Peggy Duff, put it, 'People who have large homes and businesses and who make money out of the borough must be made to pay for the filthy rotten houses we have in St Pancras.'

The Conservatives' answers about who should pay for housing were very different and they set about lowering the housing deficit in two ways. First, they began to cut the ever more costly building programme to both reduce the expense and because they simply did not share Labour's commitment to public housing. Secondly, the Tories argued that there was 'an ever widening margin' between the level of council rents in the borough and the level of private sector rents decontrolled by the Rent Act. They proposed bringing council rents into line with the free-market rents to boost council revenue. Some increase in rents was inevitable. The district auditor (the watchdog who overseas council spending) had already surcharged Labour councillors for not raising rents, and forced them to make changes. But, where Labour made modest rises to protect tenants, the Tories' primary objective was to cut the deficit. There was 'ample evidence of the need for an urgent rent review' they said, and they would not shy from the tough choices needed to push it through. The new Conservative administration produced a radical plan. It proposed rent increases that would cut the housing deficit by £175,000 per year. The Tories admitted that their proposals meant stiffer increases for some council tenants than had been faced by some private tenants under the 1957 Rent Act. But deficit reduction was the goal and this demanded the biggest possible rent increases over the shortest possible time scale.

The proposals were a bombshell for tenants. Some rents would be doubled or even trebled: the local newspaper calculated that the rent on a typical five-room flat near the town hall would more than double – from £1 8s to £3 3d per week. The Tories maintained that their proposals would produce both winners and losers. But it was clear which group most tenants would fall into. According to town hall figures, of the nearly 8,000 tenants just 3 per cent would see their rent reduced against over 60 per cent who would face an increase while the remainder would pay the same. Had the terms of the scheme been less brutal and phased in over a longer period, it would have been easier to diffuse the inevitable anger. The tenants' leader, Don Cook (*see* chapter 9), subsequently explained that 'had the Tories been less ham-fisted in their introduction to the scheme there would have been much less of a reaction from the tenants'. But reaction there was – and of a magnitude that nobody could have predicted.

Exactly how much each tenant would pay in future depended on two elements: the value of the property and an assessment of the tenant's income to work out how much they could afford to pay. The second part, the income assessment, amounted to what was known as a 'means test', and the means test was despised among the working class as a degrading method of determining welfare provision. It had been a hated method of calculating benefits during the depression of the 1930s and it was the most detested element in the scheme in St Pancras. For example, where a son or daughter remained at home with elderly parents the child might be deemed to be the tenant and the elderly occupants extra income earners. There were allowances for some groups such as young children in the home but these were limited and one rule was an eerie forerunner of the bedroom tax introduced by the 2010–15 Cameron government. Under the St Pancras scheme 'special consideration' was to be given to 'persons who choose to occupy accommodation too large for them'. In other words, no rebate would be gives to them.

The most contentious proposal was to assess not just the tenants' income but that of the tenants' spouse too, so that up to 20 per cent of a whole family's income could be taken in rent. The role of married women in the 1950s workplace was insecure and their incomes were generally helping to make ends meet or for family perks. Peggy Duff spoke for many when she attacked the proposal to include spouse income in the assessment as a 'monstrous' penalty on working women. The *New Statesman* magazine agreed and one columnist wrote:

Nothing has angered the [St Pancras] tenants more than the refusal to allow – as the successful Lambeth and Hammersmith schemes do allow – the first pound or two of a housewife's income to be left out of the calculations of family income ... Differential rents may be justified – but what is a fair rent? One eighth of income, as in Lambeth, or one fifth as in St Pancras? And how long are the Government prepared to wash its hands of the social results of high interest rates and little planning?

What constituted a fair rent was a moot point. Levels varied across London. The St Pancras Tories claimed that half of the other twenty-nine councils in London operated similar schemes to the one they proposed. They argued that better-off tenants would now pay more so that poorer tenants could pay less. Time and again, Conservatives claimed that a policy of low rents for all was merely a subsidy that allowed better-off tenants to buy luxuries like radios and TVs at the ratepayers' expense. Labour accepted that the need for some rent increases, but opposed the scale of the Tories deficit reduction. The Tory proposals were harsher even than other means-tested schemes in London and penalised middle-income earners. Labour leaders also highlighted the real problems being caused by land-price inflation in the capital. It was not, they argued, the tenants' fault that it now cost over £2,500 to put up a flat in central London and tenants could not be expected to shoulder the burden alone. Housing in areas of the capital like St Pancras were special cases and needed larger subsidies to compensate for costs of building in the area.

At 4.17 a.m. on 30 July, the mayor of St Pancras finally adjourned the council's monthly meeting. It had been a marathon session of over nine hours and, as weary councillors filed out of the council chamber, they were left to reflect on the evening's debate. Tory Leader Paul Prior had opened his speech presenting the new rent scheme with the words 'this is the most important proposal to come before the council since the war' and it was probably the last thing he said on which all sides could agree. The mayor's appeal for calm was quickly forgotten as the debate turned into a lengthy, acrimonious slanging match in which the Labour group forced eleven divisions without any success.

The Tenants Organise

As councillors traded insults across the council chamber tenants gathered outside the town hall in the first of many mass protests. The demonstration that night brought together local politicians, trade unionists and tenants' leaders who agreed to work together and two weeks later the United Tenants' Association (UTA) was launched to resist the rent scheme. The organisation was a crucial driver of the events which were about to unfold. Various officers were elected and Charles Taylor, a Fleet Street printer, became the Chair while Don Cook, an engineer, was Secretary.

These and other UTA leaders had much in common. They were all skilled working class men and all rooted in the communities they came from. They were politically experienced and understood effective organisation as trade union shop stewards or political activists; and they had known danger during the Second World War. Charlie Taylor saw active service as a naval rating on the extremely hazardous north Atlantic convoys and Don Cook was an ex-paratrooper who had fought at the Battle of Arnhem. It was Cook who emerged as the pivotal figure in the movement – quick-witted and a natural communicator, he provided the UTA with the charismatic figurehead it needed. A retired police inspector and council tenant told the *Observer* newspaper 'I've met a few people in my day and he is one of the greatest. He is a rough and ready cockney but he can write a good letter and make a fine speech. This is not just heroics – I admire every bit of him.' It was typical of the reactions that Cook inspired.

The UTA's leaders were highly political – Cook was a member of the Communist Party while Taylor had recently been expelled from the Labour Party – and this led to frequent accusations that the movement was 'communist inspired'. It was a charge denied by Cook, who attempted to present the image of a spontaneous, broad-based popular movement and claimed 'our Central Committee comprises a Conservative, two Communists and a number of Labour members of the Borough council – we have done everything possible to keep politics out of this – it is something which has got nothing to do with politics.'

That the UTA leadership had 'nothing to do with politics' was stretching the truth somewhat but so was the Tory assertion that the organisation was little more than a communist front. The truth was altogether more complex. The UTA functioned as an umbrella organisation for individual tenants' associations and grew out of the Holborn and St Pancras United Workers and Tenants' Defence Committee (UWTDC) in which many on the left – including the expelled Labour activists – had been involved (*see* chapter 6). As such, it had an off-the-peg political network ready to harness the growing tenant's frustration.

In the summer of 1959 the council estates of St Pancras buzzed with news about the new rents. Tenants shared their anxiety during street-corner chats or saloon-bar debates. Increasingly, tenants turned to the UTA leaders for guidance and they, in turn, worked tirelessly to help set up individual Tenants' Associations (TA). The results were spectacular. By September, more than thirty individual TAs across the borough representing some 7,000 tenants had been established and were affiliated to the UTA. Open weekly meetings provided forums where TA leaders, ordinary tenants and others met to discuss the campaign. Between 300 and 400 people turned up to these meetings. The UTA then had a highly efficient network for keeping tenants in touch with its decision makers: leaflets or newsletters could be turned around within twenty-four hours and, at its height, the organisation was putting out two to three leaflets per week across the council's estates.

Mass protest was the UTA's speciality. In early September 1959, it organised a march of 4,000 people to the town hall to present a petition signed by some 6,000 people protesting at the rent rises. Two weeks later, 600 tenants lobbied a meeting of the Housing Committee. The Tory leader, Paul Prior, assured them that he was determined to resolve difficulties with 'reason and tolerance' and promised that a subcommittee, comprised of Tory and Labour members, would monitor the scheme to help in cases of real hardship. But this committee never got off the ground. As it had no powers to make fundamental changes to the rent scheme, Labour refused to participate; the party was not about to be alienated from the tenants' movement by trying to help make the Tory proposals work.

When Prime Minister Harold McMillan called a general election for 8 October, the UTA seized the opportunity to make its voice heard in the national campaign. Around 4,000 people marched from St Pancras town hall to Conservative Central Office in Westminster, where the UTA leaders lobbied the Tory Party Chair, Lord Hailsham. The demonstration was covered extensively in the national press and *The Times* concluded, with studied understatement, that 'rent is still the prime issue in Holborn and St Pancras South'. Back in the constituency, Lena Jeger played up the housing issue for all it was worth – the strapline on her election manifesto warned, 'The Tory Government puts up rents for private tenants – Tory council ... proposes higher rents for council tenants – vote Labour for fair rents'. But the appeal was not enough. Like many other Labour candidates, Jeger was swept away in the Tory landslide and she lost the seat to the moderate, photogenic Tory television presenter Geoffrey Johnson-Smith. The Conservative's third successive general election victory in 1959 crushed Labour morale throughout the country. With the crisis looming over rents in St Pancras, the defeat was an especially bitter pill for the left to swallow and local activists were bewildered. As a democratic socialist party, Labour was committed to making change by winning elections and using the institutions of power. The prospect of more years slogging in opposition – both in St Pancras and Westminster – was an utterly demoralising prospect.

A week after the general election the council met again for another heated, marathon debate on the rent scheme. The Tories were cock-a-hoop with their national victory and less inclined than ever to make concessions. When Labour amendments were voted down, the opposition in the council chamber and tenants in the gallery walked out in protest. Labour's election defeat had sharpened the tenants' frustration and attitudes hardened. 'That's your lot Prior – get some police protection,' shouted one as the protesters were cleared from the public gallery of the council chamber. There was every reason for the Tory leader to take the threat seriously. Outside, over 4,000 tenants – led by a pipe and drum band – had marched to lobby the council meeting and were demonstrating noisily in the streets around the town hall. They were held back from the building by mounted police and others who had been drafted in from all over London, while another seven vans and three coach loads of reinforcements waited in the side streets. Don Cook predicted a long struggle ahead between the council and the tenants and scuffles with police ensued when he attempted to address the crowd. Things were turning ugly and the scene suggested that something was going seriously wrong with the normal run of politics in St Pancras.

Sunday 8 November 1959 was a damp autumnal day when UTA heads gathered in Kentish Town. Like the weather, the leadership was in sombre mood. The Tory administration in the town hall was determined to press on with the rent scheme and there would be no Labour government in Westminster to stop them. The UTA leaders agreed to ratchet up their opposition and call for a rent strike; when the increases were demanded in a few weeks' time, tenants simply continued to pay their rent at the existing level until the scheme was renegotiated. It sounded like a simple plan, but was actually a major step change in the campaign. A rent strike would put tenants beyond the law and, potentially, lead to evictions. The UTA gambled that if the tenants held firm it would be impossible for the council to evict thousands of people on strike. But a gamble it was, and UTA leaders knew it.

Cook understood that many tenants would be apprehensive. He played down fears of eviction and attempted to persuade tenants that they would not be fighting alone. By now the dispute was generating growing media comment and interest around the country. 'The eyes of tenants all over the country are on St Pancras,' he assured them, 'For if the Tories in this borough succeed in imposing this vicious scheme then the other boroughs will follow suit.' Exactly what support the St Pancras tenants might get was a moot point but, within the borough itself, the political temperature continued to rise.

'Extremely acrimonious ... [with] threats and taunts ... bandied about across the Council Chamber for most of its four-and-a-half-hour duration' was how the local paper reported the council meeting at the end of 1959. Council meetings now followed a familiar pattern: mass demonstrations in the streets outside the town hall and pandemonium inside, with rowdy protests both on the floor of the council chamber and in the public gallery. At the end of November, the UTA presented yet another petition, this time with 16,000 signatures. Even allowing for the inevitable forgeries and double counting it was an impressive total and twice the number of registered council tenants.

The new year of 1960 in St Pancras was ushered in with a swing. Ken Colyer was one of Britain's most popular jazz musicians, with a lively and traditional New Orleans sound that could still hold its own against the upstarts of rock 'n' roll. He was also a solid socialist who did not need to be asked twice to turn out in support of the St Pancras tenants. On 2 January the UTA organised a massive demonstration, and the column moved from estate to estate as Colyer's band thumped out the trad jazz and skiffle numbers that had made them one of the most sought-after acts in the country. When the last riff faded, however, the tenants were faced with the stark reality of the rent strike and in the middle of a propaganda war between the town hall and the UTA.

The Rent Stike Begins...

'Lower than anticipated' said a tight-lipped official from the town hall when asked exactly how many tenants had joined the strike. The UTA disagreed. It claimed that thousands of tenants had signed up for the action and were now witholding rent. Town hall sources suggested that of over 4,200 tenants faced with an increase, just 1,400 tenants had refused to pay the extra. Tory leader Paul Prior went further and claimed that only 820 declarations of non-payment (issued by the UTA) had been returned to the town hall and he contrasted this with the 'considerable rush' by tenants applying for rent assessment forms at the town hall. The UTA rubbished the council figures and said that 80 per cent of tenants were on strike. In propaganda distributed to bolster confidence it urged tenants to remain calm in the face of the council which was 'confounded and confused' by the strike.

The Tories soon began to ratchet up the pressure on the striking tenants and decided that a 'Notice to Quit' should be sent to each of the 1,100 tenants who had not paid the increases; this was the first stage of an eviction process and gave the tenant twenty-eight days to pay the arrears before the council could apply to court for an eviction order. Given the size of the resistance – evicting 1,000 tenants would have been impossible – the council faced a serious problem and the Tory leader Paul Prior was certainly feeling the pressure. The Conservative group was jittery: St Pancras was the focus of national media attention and might well end up looking like heavy-handed landlords evicting impoverished tenants (the canny UTA would be sure to highlight the neediest cases). Leaks from the Tory group suggested that the tensions threatened to undermine Prior's position as leader but in the ensuing stand-off it was the tenants who blinked first: their solidarity began to crack and many tenants began to pay up.

By the middle of February, the local newspaper headline reported 'Collapse of the Rent Strike'. According to a council spokesman, 156 Notices to Quit – the second legal stage of the eviction process – had been sent out and this prompted most recipients to pay up. This left just sixty-eight tenants on strike. The ease with which the council were able to reduce the numbers on strike from over 1,000 to just sixty-eight within a month revealed a profound difficulty for the UTA. Tenants were understandably apprehensive about losing their homes and holding the strike together in the face of eviction was a tall order. At the next council meeting, in mid-February, Labour challenged the threatened evictions but an increasingly confident Paul Prior was in no mood for compromise. He promised that all sixty-eight tenants 'would be evicted if necessary' and this led to more tenants paying up. The council subsequently announced that it needed to proceed with just twenty-three prosecutions.

The end of the rent strike was a huge blow for the UTA, which had based its entire strategy on mass action and solidarity. The tenants were apprehensive about the new rents but they were even more terrified of eviction. The UTA needed to think again. In retreat and defeated, the UTA stepped up its rowdy disruption of council business and at the council meeting in May there was bedlam in the council chamber when eggs and leaflets were showered from the balcony onto the councillors below. The gavel-banging mayor called for order and, yet again, ordered the public galleries to be cleared. This time there was a hitch. Anticipating ejection once more, some tenants had chained themselves to their seats in the public gallery and could not be removed for over an hour. The infuriated council leader, Paul Prior, complained 'we can no longer afford to have our meetings broken up like this' and moved that the public be excluded for the next three council meetings. The council would effectively now meet in secret and in defiance of the normal rules of local democracy, which would allow citizens to witness meetings.

At this, the entire Labour group walked out in protest and London Labour MPs raised the issue of public access to council meetings on the floor of the House of Commons with the local government minister, Henry Brooke. They challenged him to condemn the council for curtailing rights of local electors to observe their council. But Brooke, who had been given a very rough time by tenants when he came to speak in Holborn just a few months before, stood by his Tory colleagues and said tartly that 'it is extremely doubtful whether the demonstrators are pleasing anybody but themselves'.

The exclusion marked an abrupt suspension to ordinary norms of political decision making in St Pancras and meant that meetings were now being held in camera. But it did not end there. It now seemed as though the council was only able to function at all with the aid of a permanent police cordon to protect it. In another parliamentary intervention St Pancras North MP Kenneth Robinson asked Home Office ministers how often police had been called to the town hall between July 1959 and July 1960. He was told that up to nearly 200 extra police had been employed near St Pancras town hall on twenty-eight separate occasions (i.e. more than twice a month).

The pressure on councillors – intimidation even – did not always end at the council meetings. Paul Prior alleged that the UTA organised the harassment of Conservative councillors and their families at home and the town hall trade union, NALGO, also complained some pressure was being put on their members during the dispute. If true, this was certainly a very ugly side to the UTA campaign, but Don Cook insisted that the pressure came mainly from groups of women who descended on the homes of Conservative councillors almost every evening to demand a meeting. The targeting of politicians' homes has more recently been adopted during the economic crisis in Spain, where activist groups have protested against the eviction of those unable to pay their mortgages. Many, not least the politicians on the receiving end, have questioned the legitimacy of these actions even when no physical damage is done and it is a tactic that continues to provoke debate and controversy to this day.

The collapse of the initial rent strike in the spring of 1960 was a real setback for the UTA. The strength of feeling about the rent increases – and the rapid politicisation of many people who became involved in the protests – was obvious. But, crucially and understandably, very few of St Pancras' 8,000 tenants were prepared to face the prospect of losing their home, which was the consequence of illegal action. The UTA's inability to maintain support for direct action was a serious strategic flaw and the leaders were now forced to rethink their campaign. Instead of mass strikes the UTA now decided to challenge the council in court with three test cases.

A Singular Case

Don Cook, Arthur Rowe and Gladys Turner were all summoned to appear at Bloomsbury County Court in the summer of 1960 to explain why they should not be evicted. Lawyers sympathetic to the UTA advised Cook that, in law, the position was hopeless and there were no grounds for resisting eviction. Nevertheless, the court gave the tenants another platform and Cook decided to contest the case on the grounds that the council were being 'unreasonable' in their demand for a higher rent. The massive publicity around the case aroused the interest of the judge, Sir Alan Pugh, who decided to hear the appeal and was apparently glad that he did, for at the end of the day, he thanked Cook and remarked that he had seldom heard anyone put a case better.

That day, Cook's cross-examination of the Borough Treasurer of St Pancras (also somewhat confusingly called Cooke) and one exchange outlined the crux of the issue. Don Cook asked if some of the new maximum rents imposed by the council's new rent scheme were two or three times the levels of the old rents. Cooke agreed that this was so. Judge Pugh then asked if this was fair.

Cooke: 'Yes'.
Don Cook: 'Do you realise that if you put up the rents in my block by 7s 6d you could get rid of your subsidy [to the HRA].'

Cooke: 'Yes. But that does not make any allowance for the properties being built and those we plan to build.'

In other words, building on increasingly expensive land at ever higher interest rates was at the root of the council deficit. Without subsidies from central government, councils in central London who wanted to improve their housing stock could never escape the trap: the more the councils built, the higher rents needed to rise.

Don Cook's rhetorical skills were stronger than the legal grounds of his appeal and, while the court was bound to find against him (which it did), Judge Pugh was clearly sympathetic to the tenants. When summing up, Pugh observed that 'many tenants would find it difficult to pay the higher rents.' This was a snub to the council and although Pugh was obliged to grant an eviction order, he increased the length of time allowed to the tenants before it could be served. Following the judgement more than two hundred people staged a sit-down protest outside the town hall in support of the three, and the press coverage was massive: for the UTA the case, and Pugh's comments, were a morale-boosting propaganda victory, which confirmed that the tenants had a good case. The council, however, remained unmoved. More street protests followed and in late July even some last-ditch talks between the UTA and the town hall to try and find a compromise. But these came to nothing. The council and their tenants were now locked on to a collision course which would reach its bloody and violent climax just a few days later.

The council meeting in July was another marathon session with the debate on housing alone taking five hours. In addition to raising rents, the Tories were now slicing into the housebuilding programme and had just announced that they were shelving a scheme for 382 flats commissioned by Labour. This, inevitably, meant a longer wait for people who needed a home but the Tories had an answer for that. They now proposed that none of the 4,000 people who had joined the borough's housing waiting list should be allocated a home until the pre-1950 applicants had been cleared. 'I would sooner come out into the open,' said Paul Prior with the bluntness that was his political trademark, 'and say to those people who have been on the list for less than ten years "no, you haven't got a hope".' Leaving people without hope seldom makes for good politics and comments like this go some way to explaining why the Tory leader was so detested by many tenants during the dispute.

'An Open Declaration of War'

Tension simmered in the balmy summer days of early September. The eviction notices granted by the court expired on 28 August, which meant that bailiffs could now physically repossess the flats occupied by Cook and Rowe at any time. Roy Orbison's smash hit 'Only the Lonely' climbed up the singles charts, but the two tenants in St Pancras were anything but isolated. Cook's flat in Kentish Town and Rowe's flat in Regent's Park were headline news across the country and looked more like sets from a film about the Second World War than council flats. Both were surrounded by barbed wire and guarded by twenty-four-hour pickets made up of men, women and children. Within, the flats were now shored up with wooden partitions and heavy objects to obstruct eviction – twelve pianos had been hauled into Cook's flat – so that physically removing the two tenants was not going to be straightforward even for burly bailiffs practised in their work. Physically, the eviction looked as though it was going to be rough, but, for an Arnhem veteran like Cook there was really little to fear.

'Whilst both the Borough Council and the UTA express themselves as willing to negotiate both appear willing to fight on to the bitter end if need be,' said the local paper. Violence, it seemed, would be the inevitable conclusion to the confrontation. Tory council chiefs now steadfastly refused to even meet with the tenants and said that they would only talk when the arrears were paid up and the barricades had come down. Some suspected that an element of macho-politics had entered into the crisis and Peggy Duff was not the only one who saw the dispute as an increasingly personal battle between Don Cook and Paul Prior. Several last-ditch attempts at mediation by others were made – and failed. The London group of Labour MPs, led by the former docker and Bermondsey MP Bob Mellish, met the housing minister, Henry Brooke, but talks broke down after ninety minutes. With his typical bullishness, Mellish declared, 'We regard this now as an open declaration of war' – a form of words that surely did little to calm the situation.

On 21 September, the UTA organised a mass lobby of the St Pancras Housing Committee and that evening the already volatile atmosphere erupted into violence that lasted for two days. Police, who had previously banned demonstrations from the vicinity of the town hall, now used mounted officers to clear demonstrators from the area; 'St Pancras Crowd Charged by Mounties' screamed the *Daily Mirror* front-page headline, and the crowd reacted angrily. 'The police action turned a peaceful demonstration into an angry mob,' Charles Taylor and Alderman Charles Taylor, the UTA Chair, told the *Financial Times*. Certainly, the use of horses against a crowd, which included women and children, further inflamed local opinion and attracted sympathy to the tenants. Eleven arrests were made that night, including former council leader John Lawrence, who was subsequently jailed for three months. Other important figures in the tenants' organisation were also detained and having defenestrated the tenant's leadership, police and bailiffs now moved swiftly to finish their task.

Just before dawn on 22 September 1960, a massive police operation began around the flats in Kentish Town and Regent's Park. Fireworks, bells and whistles were meant to alert tenants' reinforcement, but by the time many people arrived – some in their pyjamas – it was too late. Hundreds of police surrounded the two blocks. Despite being pelted with bricks and bottles, they held the mass of angry tenants at bay until bailiffs could batter their way into the properties. At Silverdale House they simply knocked a 7-foot-high hole in the external wall of Arthur Rowe's home, and entered without difficulty. Resistance was fiercest at Cook's flat. Police were pelted with coins by tenants who told them to 'go and buy some medals' while bailiffs moved in behind them to smash their way through the ceiling. Soaked with engine oil, which had been poured on them from the roof, it then took the bailiffs one and a half hours to break their way through the barricaded interior. They eventually cornered Don Cook, who was with a friend in the kitchen brewing tea. Cook invited the bailiffs to join them for a cuppa; this was, after all, a very British eviction.

'The Tory council in St Pancras now stands condemned as the instigators of the most violent attack on ordinary people for many years,' proclaimed Cook when he finally emerged from the remains of his home later in the day. 'Arthur Rowe and I are out of our flats but there are many more who will follow us. The barricades of St Pancras have only just begun. We will continue to fight and justice must prevail.' These were brave, bold words but ultimately futile. They could not disguise the reality that Cook and Rowe were out, defeated. Worse still, the UTA now appeared to have no strategy. The message was aimed at bolstering morale but begged more questions than answers: what, exactly would the UTA do next and what leadership could it offer the tenants now? In fact, the UTA had no Plan B.

The lack of strategy soon revealed itself as a serious problem because the UTA was fast losing control of events. After some febrile discussion it was decided to organise a march from Cook's now ex-flat in Kentish Town to the town hall. Quite what the object was no one seemed clear, but that evening many hundreds of people set off from Kentish Town for St Pancras and they were joined by many more along the way. By the time the column reached the back of St Pancras station, up to 14,000 people were on the street, only to find their way blocked by lines of police at the top of Midland Road, some quarter of a mile from the town hall. Having embarked on a course of direct action it was difficult to halt the momentum, and the confrontation that followed rapidly turned into a pitched battle.

When it came to apportion blame as to who started it, fingers pointed in all directions. 'Speaker after speaker called for violence when just one or two moderating voices might have made all the difference,' recalled Peggy Duff of the tenants' march. Other witnesses thought the police were responsible. Anthony Curragh of the *Daily Herald* described how 'The police action ... was the worst and most frightening I have ever seen ... Quite unnecessarily I was pushed and kicked and sent hurtling against a wall by policemen who, in my opinion, had completely lost their tempers. There was no simple request to "move on", they just came at us with fists flying.'

What everyone agreed on was the shocking level of violence. Another *Herald* reported confirmed that 'at times the savagery of the fighting seemed unbelievable.' *Daily Express* reporter Clifford Luton sheltered in a phone booth in St Pancras station to file his copy while police fought with men and women on the concourse outside:

> Hundreds of police have just charged a crowd in the Euston Road and are locked face to face in the most vicious fighting I have yet seen. I heard dozens of women screaming as they went down ... It was a nightmare of confusion of flying fists and boots. Unconscious men, blood streaming from their faces were dragged across the streets. Five policemen at a time manhandled rioters behind their cordon. In the pouring rain lay a woman's white shoe ... a handbag ... the torn sleeve of a jacket ... a pair of shattered spectacles. Someone picked up a policeman's helmet. Immediately four policemen grabbed him, threw him down. His head hit the pavement.

The Home Secretary subsequently stated that sixteen policemen were injured, some seriously. There are no records of the protestors who were injured but forty-four were charged and appeared in a special session at Clerkenwell Court the next day.

The violence in St Pancras stunned the nation. Newsreels whirred with images of the affray in cinemas around the country and it was on the front page of almost every national newspaper. Lurid headlines such as 'Now the Bloodshed – Police Mauled in Night Battle' or 'St Pancras Mob Attack 300 Police' and 'Fury of St Pancras – 1,000 Police Charge' were not what people expected to read over their breakfast tea and toast in a country where, according to the prime minister, people had never had it so good. 'A rowdy procession ... shouting offensive and inflammatory remarks' was how the otherwise unflappable Butler described the St Pancras tenants. Challenged by local MP Kenneth Robinson on the floor of the House of Commons about the breakdown of law and order, Butler defended the police and blamed the tenants. No one could be sure where events might lead next but a horrified Butler was taking no chances and rapidly invoked Section 3 of the Public Order Act (1936). This draconian piece of legislation had originally been passed to keep Oswald Mosley's British Union of Fascists off the streets and stop them causing mayhem before the war. It had not been needed for more than a decade until it was dusted down and used in St Pancras – the only time that the population of an entire London borough has been subject to an order under the Act. It effectively curtailed the right of free association even for two or more people on the street and, from 6 p.m. on 23 September 1960, all demonstrations in the borough were banned for three months. Butler's approach left opinions divided. 'The hooliganism in St Pancras must be sternly suppressed. It is an outrageous outburst of unjustified indignation which deserves no sympathy. No responsible politician will allay himself with the rioters,' opined the *News Chronicle*, and similar views were repeated across the right-wing media. Others were less sure and, while not excusing the violence, thought that the causes went deeper than just rowdy tenants.

'"Cease Fire!" – St Pancras is not the Congo,' demanded the *Daily Mirror* editorial in a comparison with the African state, which was being pulled apart by intercommunal violence. The paper wanted answers to three key questions: 'Were the police too tough? Were the tenants too stubborn? Did St Pancras Borough Council make a grave mistake?' The answer was almost certainly 'yes' to all three questions. But the *Mirror* did not seek an instant verdict, rather it asked for a period of cool reflection with time to work out what had gone so terribly wrong. The National Council for Civil Liberties took up the challenge of investigating the melee, while the political parties and UTA were left to lick their wounds and work out how to re-establish normal politics in the borough – if that were possible

Dealing with the riots as a security issue was easier than finding a way of defusing the political tensions. Tory council leaders were, like many people across Britain, shaken by the events of the previous forty-eight hours, which had escalated beyond what anyone had expected. Chastened and under pressure from Labour, the council offered to reopen talks with the UTA, but within a few days some in the tenants' organisation were advocating the resumption of a rent strike. The Tories were furious at what they regarded as a breach of good faith and even the Labour leader Ratchford described the UTA move as 'a stab in the back' for his efforts to find a conciliated settlement. In fact, some in the UTA would have agreed with Ratchford and, whispered very softly, even with the Tories.

There was a power struggle going on in within the association. As the tenants tried to plan the best way forward, differing factions fought for ascendency. Just days after the riots, a decisive meeting was held where the differences were debated and a new realism seems to have suffused the meeting. As usual, Peggy Duff was involved and recalled, 'John Lawrence was there. He wanted, as usual, to challenge the state, to defy the ban on demonstrations. This was he thought the beginning of a revolution.' Other important voices were less sure, notably the Communist Party which had begun to distance itself from Cook and other local members. The CP hierarchy was by now increasingly cautious and much more careful. The label 'adventurism' had yet to enter the communist lexicon but it is what the party now thought about the rebels.

In the end, no precise decision was taken about ending the protest. Gradually the situation deflated and the temperature dropped. Some tenants went on refusing to pay the increases while others paid up gradually through gritted teeth. For their part, the Tories offered a limited modification of the scheme with marginal changes involving a loss of rent revenue of around £15,000 – the equivalent of a 1d increase on the rates. By the end of November, the newspaper headline announced: 'Rent War Fades as Tenants Pay Up.'

'Fighting in a Different Way'

In effect the Tories had won the battle of St Pancras. Cook and Rowe were genuine working-class heroes. They attracted media interest across the nation. They were ahead of their time and drew attention to the plight of those trapped in the dysfunctional London housing market three years before the Rachman scandal broke. They inspired legendary folk musicians like Ewan MacColl and Peggy Seeger to compose one of their best songs, but it is important not to confuse means and ends. The folk songs, mass marches and crowded meetings were only the means. The prized goal was to change the Tory rent scheme and in that crucial objective the protests failed. A handful of tenants refused to pay increases but despite Don Cook's promise on the day of his eviction that the barricades of St Pancras would continue there was little enthusiasm for more resistance. Cook recognised this more clearly than some and argued for a new approach. In February 1961 he told a mass meeting of the UTA that 'We must work to see that there is a defeat for the Tories in the LCC elections and, above all, we have got to work for the return of a Labour Council next year. We are not withdrawing from the battle. We are going to fight it in a different way.' What he did not say, but what he meant, was that the only viable option for tenants was that of democratic socialism rather than a quasi-revolutionary mass movement.

The UTA's new approach effectively vindicated Labour's position from the start of the dispute. In the volatile atmosphere of the conflict Labour's insistence on constitutional channels of opposition through the town hall had looked irrelevant and lost some traction. Other voices advocating direct action had a far more potent appeal to the thousands of tenants facing hefty rent increases. The tenants' anger combined with the communist-influenced UTA leadership meant that the conventional ways of doing politics in the area, and the ordinary democratic forums to resolve tensions were put under tremendous pressure. The nature of the challenge for Labour to stay within the law was clear from the outset, as just one example showed. Soon after the rent scheme was announced, Labour convened a meeting of tenants at the Unity Theatre in the heart of working-class King's Cross. It was a difficult evening for the Labour politicians. The local press reported how 'suggestions from the platform that only legal means should be adopted were received with a marked lack of enthusiasm. Demands from speakers from the floor that there should be an all-out fight, including if necessary a refusal to fill out forms and even a rent strike, met with vociferous approval.' Labour needed a carefully crafted response: standing shoulder to shoulder with the tenants, while rejecting revolutionary politics.

Local party members – many of whom were council tenants – participated fully in all of the legal demonstrations organised by the UTA. They debated endlessly how far the party would engage with the fight against evictions when they came; sometimes the local party seemed committed to 'physical resistance' and at other times just 'practical assistance' or even 'moral resistance'. Party members were encouraged to support the pickets protecting Cook and Rowe but not, apparently, take part in any physical action when the police and bailiffs arrived. It was a fine line for Labour to tread and there were strong opinions on both sides about how far party members should challenge the law. In any event, most ordinary members made up their own minds about what they were prepared to do or not do.

The independent socialists who had just been expelled from the Labour Party, on the other hand, had no compunction about breaking the law and were in the vanguard of those calling for direct action. Together with the local Communist Party, they were both prepared to organise and participate in whatever it took to defeat the Tory proposals, even if that meant illegality. Labour fought the new rent scheme with unusual tenacity in the council chamber and used every tactic it could think of. But, in the end, it would not support illegal methods because, logically, a party committed to constitutional democracy cannot have it both ways.

After the collapse of the strike and the evictions, Labour capitalised on the tenants' traditional loyalties to the party and encouraged UTA members to become active at a local level. On a more formal basis, links between the UTA and the Labour Party were cemented; party leaders began to meet with UTA leaders in early 1961 and the relationship flourished. 'We want your help to ensure the return of a Labour Council next May,' a Labour councillor told the crowd at a rally to mark the anniversary of the evictions, in September 1961. He promised that Labour was 'in close touch with the UTA to try and work out a satisfactory solution to the rents problem.' That solution was announced a few months later.

Early in 1962, with UTA approval, Labour proposed to replace the differential, means-tested rents with standard, flat-rate rents. A few months later, the party regained control of St Pancras Council at the local elections and the Labour leader acknowledged the importance of the tenants' support in making the victory happen. He promised that 'there will be some big changes on policy straight away. The differential rents scheme will be abolished. That was the issue on which the electorate voted us into power.'

The new rent proposals were conspicuous by their absence, however. The Labour administration was told that the cost of the scheme – an estimated £100,000 extra to the council's budget – would again bring them into trouble with the district auditor. It was impossible to introduce without embarking, once again, on the saga of surcharging and disqualifications experienced in 1957–59. According to Peggy Duff, the councillors discovered that a differential rent scheme, once adopted 'could ... not be abandoned without further surcharge on the councillors. The district auditor in fact controlled the level of council rents, not the councillors, nor the citizens who elected them.'

Because of these constraints, Labour were only able to make marginal changes involving an aggregate reduction of £20,000 – a lot less that the £100,000 planned for and promised. Duff claimed that the frustrated councillors tried to raise the issue with both the Ministry of Housing, local government and the national Labour Party but, she complained, 'neither ever showed a spark of response'. The battle of rents in St Pancras finished, in the end, with both a bang and a whimper.

Chapter 8

EPILOGUE

In October 1964, the photographers' flashbulbs popped as a grinning Harold Wilson stood on the steps of No. 10 Downing Street to acknowledge the cheers of his supporters. He was the first Labour prime minister for thirteen years. After more than a decade in opposition, in which the furious debates about housing, the 1957 Rent Act and the Rachman scandal had featured so prominently, Labour might have been expected to have detailed policy proposals ready to go. But, as the new housing minister Richard Crossman recorded in his diary, it was not quite the flying start he had expected.

Labour in Power – 'That's All There Is'

Crossman arrived at his office on the first day, full of enthusiasm to get on with the job. The new government hurriedly prepared the queen's speech and 'the main preoccupation for the department ... my main job in the legislative programme ... would be to introduce a big measure for reasserting rent control.' But Crossman was deflated to discover that hardly any planning or thought had gone into what should happen.

> Characteristically enough, I find that though for five years the Labour Party has been committed to the repeal of the Henry Brooke Rent Act there is only one slim series of notes by Michael

Stewart [the party's housing spokesman in opposition] on the kind of way to do it in Transport House [Labour's Head Office]. That's all there is.

One academic study of housing in the post-war period echoed Crossman's disappointment and concluded that 'Labour seemed to have almost as much difficulty about formulating a housing policy in this period as they did with defence or nationalisation'. The party was committed to a policy of 'municipalising' housing stock, although 'what this would have meant in practice is unclear'.

Given the scale of what needed to be done and the length of time Labour had had to formulate policy, the new minister had every right to expect a more detailed brief from his own party, but worse was to follow because Crossman immediately became embroiled in one of Whitehall's classic battles between an elected politician and a Whitehall mandarin. His conflict was not with a Sir Humphrey but one of the few female permanent secretaries, Dame Evelyn Sharp. The stand-off between the two is legendary: Crossman, an Oxford double first often accused of being an intellectual bully, met his match. 'The person who dominates all proceedings is, of course, Evelyn Sharpe ... A biggish woman, about five foot ten, with tremendous blue eyes which look right through you,' he confided to his diary. Although past retirement age, Sharpe had been the mandarin in charge of housing for more than a decade and could not bear to leave her post. In the early days of the government, the hapless Crossman allowed control over planning to slip into the portfolio of another minister. As soon as she became aware of what had happened, Dame Evelyn sprang into action to reverse the decision, restore the powers 'and save her department from my stupidity and ignorance' wrote Crossman. After that, Dame Evelyn lost confidence in her minister, who found himself increasingly isolated within his own department. Crossman's red boxes emptied of decisions for him to take or things to do. After a month in office, for example, he recorded disconsolately in his diary that after one early morning meeting,

> For the rest of the day I found myself virtually unemployed as far as the Ministry was concerned. There were quite literally no engagements for me ... I had been increasingly uneasy about the absence of work for me to do and this was too much.

Crossman stalked off to the Commons, where he sat on the front bench and occupied himself by listening to a debate before returning home that evening 'deeply depressed'.

Nevertheless, the pace quickened at the ministry and housing became a government priority, especially in London. In 1965, a comprehensive survey (the Milner Holland Report) detailed shortfalls in the capital's housing and provided an extra stimulus to take action. Far from the market mechanism solving London's housing problems, as Conservative ministers had promised during the debates on the 1957 Rent Act, the report identified 'an acute shortage of rented housing in London and many difficulties and hardships arising from it'. Milner Holland's audit revealed that 190,000 London households were in urgent need of rehousing whilst around 61,000 single people lacked proper accommodation. These were truths that the Tories struggled even to acknowledge at the time but which Labour was prepared to act on. It is fashionable to carp about the failures of the Wilson government now, but its record on housing puts more recent governments to shame. One of the first measures the new government took was to repeal the 1957 Rent Act so that private tenants once again had better protection and controlled rents. Hatred of the Act ran so deep that Labour continued to use it as a dividing line between them and the Tories for years afterwards. Shortly before the 1970 election, Harold Wilson reminded people that the Tories were 'the party of the Rent Act, the landlords' party which let Rachmanism flourish'. This was not mere politicking; in his memoirs, Wilson described the Rent Act as 'odious' and his government's reining in the forces of the free market was a real relief for millions of people living in privately rented homes.

The Wilson government made major improvements to public housing too. Despite the lack of detailed plans in opposition, Labour put house building at the top of the political agenda. Within a year of Wilson entering Downing Street, the newly established Crown Lands Commission began to buy up land for community use, and the amount of money available to local authorities at special low interest rates doubled. In 1964, when Wilson took office, the average subsidy from central government to a local authority for the building of a house was £24. By 1967 it was £85. In other words, the cuts to subsidies that crippled local authorities like St Pancras were largely restored. With this encouragement, the proportion of public housing as a percentage of all new housing also rose steeply in the Wilson years and as a consequence the number of council homes built climbed steadily: 119,000 in 1964, 133,000 in 1965 and 142,000 in 1966. In total, by the end of his second term in 1970, the Wilson government had added some 2 million new homes to Britain's housing stock. True, mistakes were made in areas like architecture and planning. But they were mistakes born from a passion about housing, to experiment and to find out what would work and what didn't. Some excellent municipal housing was built in the 1960s and hundreds of thousands of people led better, healthier and happier lives as a result. They were a testament to the power of political decisions to make change happen. There were fears at the time that if and when the Conservatives returned to power all Labour's plans would be curtailed and then rolled back.

Selsdon Man: Born in St Pancras

At a speech in St Pancras (by now Camden) town hall in 1970, Wilson announced the birth of a new political figure on the British political scene. He spoke of 'Selsdon Man' who had been born following a series of Tory policy seminars at the plush Selsdon Park Hotel in Surrey. The aim of the seminars was to reinvigorate Conservative policy with a more free-market approach and Wilson's fictional character entered the political lexicon. Wilson warned that Selsdon Man was 'designing a society for the ruthless and a policy for the uncaring'. His message is 'you're out on your own'. Selsdon Man had a four-point programme, one of which, said Wilson, was 'to firm up rents in a free-for-all in housing'. In fact, although the Conservatives won the 1970 election, the life of Selsdon Man was remarkably short. The new prime minister, Edward Heath, was forced into a series of policy U-turns and retreated from his free-market election manifesto, including on housing. In his memoirs, Heath looked back with satisfaction on the housing record of his government between 1970 and 1974. It was not without controversy, but there were over 2 million housing new starts in just three years and, wrote Heath, 'In 1972, to take just one example, over a quarter of a million better homes were provided in the public sector.' These figures are eye-watering when compared to the modern record and it is hard to think of a politician – left or right – who would boast of adding 250,000 improved council homes in one year to Britain's housing stock.

Public pressure and political action to think again in these terms is long overdue because Selsdon Man has returned with a vengeance. The housing crisis in London is, once more, acute. Some of the reasons are slightly different to the 1950s, but not all. Overseas investors, inflated salaries and bonuses in the financial sector (despite the 2008 crash), population expansion, and the forced sale of council houses are all new trends. But, the root of the problem of housing in London remains and is in many ways same: an over-dependence on market forces to provide housing. Markets can be highly efficient mechanisms for sorting out who gets what when demand is based on wants; they may be far less successful when allocating resources where demand is based on basic need, as is, for example, the case with services such as policing, health or housing. A free market without corrections and stabilisers in housing simply does not work for many people in the capital. The story of the St Pancras rent riots is yet more evidence that it seldom has, or that it ever will. Unfortunately, the current Conservative government (2016) appears determined to plough on regardless of the facts on the ground. Far from heeding the evidence or lessons of history, it is estimated by housing experts that new legislation will strip up to 350,000 homes out of the public sector over the next few years. The clue as to why the Conservatives might want to go down this path was helpfully provided by the former Tory Chancellor George Osborne. During the coalition government of 2010–15, Osborne confided to Liberal Democrat leader Nick Clegg his view that 'social housing makes for Labour voters'.

This candid view brings us to conclusions about the role of the Labour Party during the St Pancras story, and today. The challenges posed by housing are among those that beg an essential, perhaps existential, question for Labour: what kind of party is it and what is it for?

It is quite clear that the root cause of the housing crisis in London and the St Pancras riots of 1960 were not left-wing firebrands but the ideology of the free market. It is equally clear that Labour's response in St Pancras under John Lawrence was ineffective. Lawrence's form of quasi-revolutionary politics did not put St Pancras Council in the vanguard of the working class. Political gestures, such as the scrapping of the mayoral allowance or the raising of the Red Flag, were not followed by other authorities. There was widespread concern about the nuclear threat, but no other council abandoned its statutory duty to provide civil defence. When Lawrence urged his fellow councillors to challenge the law with the plea that 'there will be trouble but it will be glorious trouble', they rightly saw only trouble and abandoned the policy. The euphoric mass meetings and demonstrations generated energy and enthusiasm, but not votes. The aim of effective politics is not to make a lot of noise in the world but to change it, and the most damning verdict of all on the politics of John Lawrence was delivered by the very working-class electorate in St Pancras that he sought to lead. When he and the other rebel councillors stood as Communist Party candidates they trailed humiliatingly behind the Conservatives. As it turned out, the rebel councillors needed Labour more than Labour needed them.

St Pancras's clash with national government was not unique. Over the years there have been sporadic attempts by local authorities to challenge laws passed in Westminster. Poplar in the 1920s, St Pancras in the 1950s, Clay Cross (Derbyshire) in the 1970s, or the protests against rate-capping in London and Liverpool in the 1980s are all examples. And they have all ended in failure. For good or ill, local government in Britain functions largely in the shadow of national government. European neighbours like France, Germany or Spain have powerful regional governments but, despite steps toward devolution, English councils are weak by comparison. Vigorous debate about the powers and structure of local government is essential but as the vast majority of councillors well know, public service can only be effectively performed within a democratic framework and constitutional law.

The founders of the Labour Party understood this. In 1918, Labour made a conscious decision to become a democratic socialist party. It consistently rebuffed approaches from other parties and groups that sought more revolutionary means; Labour succeeded where other parties failed. The high tide of communism in Britain was the election of 1945 when just over 100,000 (0.4 per cent of the electorate) voted for the Communist Party, giving them two parliamentary seats. The subsequent decline was swift. In 1950 they lost both the seats and by 1951 their vote collapsed to 21,000. Continental Europe produced mass-communist parties and raging debates between Marxist intellectuals in the 1950s, but these things were largely absent in Britain. Here, at least, Labour's pursuit of welfare capitalism – reform rather than revolution – was always the more attractive. There was never any equivalent of McCarthyism during the 1950s, either in the UK or in the Labour Party, largely because there was never any need. The Communist Party sounded its own death knell. In St Pancras, Lawrence and those around him tried to portray themselves as radical, but they weren't. Radical politics succeed when they frame the terms of the debate so effectively that the premises of the discussion are no longer challenged. Radical politics are bound up with the power to take action and change people's lives. Clement Attlee and Harold Wilson were radicals, not John Lawrence. If the Labour Party today is serious about transforming Britain for the better, the lessons from St Pancras are clear.

Chapter 9

CAST OF CHARACTERS

We live in an age when public life is dominated by two-dimensional politicians: our parliaments and town halls are inhabited by an elite of former special advisers and others who have never had a proper job, who know little of the world outside the corridors of power. Or, at least, that's what we are told. No such description could be levelled at any of the characters behind the events described in this book. Unfortunately there is no space to include a potted biography of them all, but even these 'brief lives' help to explain the kind of people who drove the St Pancras story. Truly, they were a remarkable generation who lived through the most testing of times.

Don Cook

Blessed with film-star good looks and natural eloquence, Don Cook made for a highly charismatic leader of the St Pancras United Tenants' Association (UTA), which organised around 8,000 council tenants in the borough. There was a lot more to Cook than just a flashing smile and memorable phrase though. During the Second World War, Cook had served as a corporal with the Parachute Regiment and had taken part in Operation Market Garden. It was an audacious plan intended to end the war by Christmas 1944, but turned into one of the most catastrophic Allied failures of the war and was better known as Arnhem (the episode was immortalised on screen by the blockbusting film *A Bridge Too Far*). Parachuted onto enemy-occupied territory across the River Rhine, Cook was one of thousands of Allied soldiers stranded for days while surrounded by crack troops from a German Panzer division. Some 14,000 British troops lost their lives in the operation – Cook being one of the lucky few who survived. After the war he returned to civilian life and worked as an engineer. But, like millions of others, Cook was no longer prepared to accept pre-war norms. Having put his life on the line for the country, he was in the vanguard of those demanding a better life for themselves and their families as Britain emerged from the Second World War.

John Lawrence

In St Pancras town hall today, the marble corridors are lined with plaques inscribed with the names of former mayors, council leaders and other assorted bigwigs who have graced the building over the years. But, strangely, there is no mention anywhere of John Lawrence, once Labour leader of St Pancras Council. More importantly still, a veil of secrecy is still tightly drawn by the Home Office. Despite repeated requests under the Freedom of Information Act, the Home Office refuse to release any details about the former leader of St Pancras Council on the grounds that – sixty years after the events described here – to do so would prejudice national security. This is odd because Lawrence was a local politician who acquired a national profile and, in his day, one of the most famous leaders St Pancras (now Camden) Council has ever had. One weekly magazine ran a profile of him under the headline 'The Amazing Mr Lawrence' while the *North London Press*, a savage critic of Lawrence's policies, nevertheless conceded that he was 'a born leader, with a charm and sincerity which have caused revolutions in lesser countries than our own'.

Lawrence had made his own way in the world: his mother, a domestic servant, died when he was an infant and his father, an army sergeant, died a few years later. Lawrence was largely brought up in a military orphanage, a miserable experience where harsh discipline and bullying were rife. He found two consolations: sport and music, and he excelled at both. He learned to play the trombone and won an army scholarship to the Royal College of Music where Gustav Holst (a fellow trombonist) and Ralph Vaughan Williams commended his talent. But it was politics which really moved him. During the 1930s he was stationed in Liverpool, and saw at first hand the misery caused by the depression and mass unemployment. The experience led him into liaisons with various radical, left-wing groups while he eked out a living as a professional musician in the orchestra pits of London's finest theatres, music halls and opera houses. Ironically, given his years in the army, a heart condition rendered him unfit for military service when war came; Lawrence spent most of the 1940s engaged in seemingly endless quarrels within the factions of the Trotskyist left. He only joined the Labour Party in the late 1940s when he moved to St Pancras, but swiftly rose up through the party where he was a high profile and controversial figure. He became council leader in 1956 and under his stewardship St Pancras adopted a set of policies that attracted the full glare of national media attention, leading to conflict with the Tory government and some local activists (*see* chapter 2). John Lawrence died in 2002 aged eighty-seven.

Peggy Duff

According to the world-renowned philosopher Noam Chomsky, Peggy Duff was 'one of the people who really changed modern history ... she should have won the Nobel Peace Prize about 20 times'. In his seminal book on the 1950s, *Having It So Good*, Professor Peter Hennessy describes her simply as 'an ace campaigner'. When her husband was killed in Burma in 1943, Duff was left to raise their three young children alone. She was an inveterate politician and first became involved in politics at the University of London, where she read English. She then worked closely with left-wing publisher Victor Gollancz on a number of campaigns from the safe repatriation of German prisoners after the war to the abolition of the death penalty. She was business manager of the *Tribune* newspaper between 1949 and 1955 – a period when it had an unsurpassed influence in the Labour Party – and this brought her into close contact with leading figures on the left: Aneurin Bevan, Michael Foot and Fenner Brockway were among her many friends. In the late 1950s Duff became a founder and Organising Secretary of the Campaign for Nuclear Disarmament (CND) and continued to work tirelessly for leftist campaigns throughout the 1960s. She was elected to St Pancras Council in 1956, where she became chief whip and tried to maintain a sense of unity among the fractured Labour group.

Louis Bondy

Small, bald and bespectacled, Louis Bondy was a man of many parts. Born into a cultured Jewish family in Berlin, Bondy trained as an architect but left Germany in 1934 soon after the Nazis came to power. After Hitler fell, he returned to Germany as a journalist for the daily newspaper *Deutsche Allgemeine Zeitung* and was an observer at the Nuremburg Trials; he penned an account of his experiences in a book called *Racketeers of Hatred* about Julius Streicher and other Nazi Jew-baiters. Like many other émigrés, however, London had become his real home and Bondy founded one of the bookshops around the British Museum, which contribute to the area's bohemian character. His speciality was miniature books and antiquarian pornography; he was an expert in both to such an extent that *Pathé News* ran a special documentary feature about his work. Bondy was also very involved in Labour politics. He was active in the Holborn and St Pancras Labour Party as a staunch ally of John Lawrence and elected to represent the area on the LCC in 1958. He continued as a GLC councillor until 1981 and was Chair of the Historic Buildings Board.

Irene Chaplin

Under 5 feet tall, Irene Chaplin's (née Marcousé) diminutive stature was in inverse relationship to her fierce intelligence and energy and zeal. A Russian Jew, she was born in Vilna (now in Lithuania). The family left in 1905 to escape the botched revolution and pogroms, first to Antwerp and then to England. She was educated in London and at one of Europe's most ancient universities, Heidelberg in southern Germany, just as a fellow student, Joseph Goebbels, was putting the finish touches to his doctorate there. Chaplin settled in Holborn in the 1930s, became a business executive and married Hugh Chaplin, Principal Keeper of the British Museum's printed book collection. The Chaplins lived in their small, book-filled, bohemian flat on the top floor of No. 44 Russell Square where a stream of visitors included International Brigade volunteers returning from the Spanish Civil War to future Labour leader Harold Wilson. 'Stick-in-the-mud' was how Irene initially described the Labour Party, but her husband persuaded her to join it in the mid-1930s at around the same time that she became a British national. In 1945, Chaplin stood as the Labour candidate in the Tory bastion of Holborn which, for the last time, had its own parliamentary seat and was still very much controlled by commerce. In those days, owners of a business were allowed two votes: one where they lived and one for the registered address of their business. This 'business vote' ensured Tory control of Holborn even though few of their electors were residents – just six of the forty-six-strong Tory group on the council actually lived in the borough. Chaplin narrowly lost the parliamentary seat to Max Aitken, son and heir of newspaper magnate Lord Beaverbrook. Labour won control of Holborn council, however, and Irene became Leader and Chair of the Housing Committee. For the next four years she threw herself into work for the homeless. Local authorities were allowed to requisition – take over – empty properties to house people left homeless by the Blitz. Chaplin set about the task with zeal. House by house she went, through the smart streets of Bloomsbury, armed only with a hammer, a bag of nails and handfuls of requisition notices to wage her war against homelessness. Pinning the notices to the doors of empty properties, she claimed them for families who needed a roof over their heads (*see* chapter 4). Labour lost control of Holborn Council in 1949. She remained active in Labour London politics as a member of the GLC and ILEA until 1977.

Tom Barker

The mayor of St Pancras, Barker's first job after leaving school was as a farm hand in his native Cumbria. He was aged eleven. As a teenager he took the king's shilling and joined the British Army but subsequently emigrated to Australia, where he was imprisoned for leading agitation against Australian involvement in the Second World War (Barker's pivotal role in the objector movement was the subject of an Australian Broadcasting Corporation documentary broadcast on national television in 2015). Protests and strikes were organised to campaign for his release with one strike leader promising that 'it will cost the capitalist class $10,000 for every day that Tom Barker remains in jail'. The Australian authorities decided on a cheaper option and had Barker deported to Chile; he was then expelled from Santiago too and ended up in Argentina, working on the docks in Buenos Aires. In the early 1920s he married a Polish ballet dancer called Berta and went to the USSR, where he worked voluntarily in Siberia helping the Soviets import heavy industrial plant (he spoke fluent Russian). He refused, however, to join the Communist Party and this complication ruffled feathers which were only smoothed by the personal intervention of both Lenin and Trotsky. He returned to the UK where – perhaps the most extraordinary career move of all given his turbulent life – he worked in London as a clerk for the London Electricity Board while he cared for his wife who had been blinded. He was a St Pancras councillor between 1949 and 1959 and his successful proposal to fly the Red Flag from the roof of the town hall attracted nationwide publicity (*see* Chapter 3).

George and Irene Wagner

These two émigrés from Nazi Germany met in London just before the war; Gyuri (or George) was a social democrat from Danzig and Irene came from a secular Jewish family living in Dresden. They married within weeks of being introduced and formed a solid partnership for more than fifty years. Irene wanted to study chemistry like her father, but by the mid-1930s National Socialism put a stop to her dream. She became active in the anti-Nazi resistance, smuggling clandestine propaganda in her underwear, before the family fled Germany shortly before the Kristallnacht. Through friends in London, Irene found a job with Peggy and Douglas Jay (a Labour MP), looking after their infant son Peter (who went on to become British ambassador in Washington). The couple spent the war working for British intelligence near Bletchley Park and when peace came they settled in Holborn. George, a cultured, pipe-smoking intellectual, was a university lecturer and local councillor while the feisty Irene worked as a librarian (she later became the Labour Party archivist). The Wagners were at the centre of local opposition to John Lawrence in the 1950s and were active in Labour politics throughout their lives.

Barry Bucknell

A Labour councillor in St Pancras who was passionate about housing from a slightly different perspective. Bucknell, a television expert on housing and home improvement, was one of the best-known faces in the country – his programme *Barry Bucknell's Do It Yourself* had over 7 million viewers. Broadcast live, the episodes were a reminder of the hazards faced by programme makers in the early years of television: the results were sometimes calamitous as his constructions collapsed or the wallpaper sagged. Normally these disappointments were met with cheery stoicism and chippy 'Well – that's not the way to do it!' Frustration and irritation with mishaps did occasionally surface, however, and this led him to another pioneering moment: he was the first person to use a four-letter word on TV when he exclaimed 'c*nt!' as a miss-hit nail went flying.

Clive Jenkins

A Labour councillor in St Pancras from south Wales renowned for his oratory, wit and style, Jenkins, who left school at fourteen, worked his way up through a series of laboratory jobs and into management. A card-carrying member of the Communist Party, he also rose up in the trade-union movement, and then combined the two successful careers by becoming General Secretary of the white-collar managerial union ASTMS. Jenkins loved the media spotlight and was a master of the soundbite before the phrase had ever been invented. Loved and loathed in equal measure, he became a much invited guest on television chat shows and a frequent newspaper columnist. In his 'Who's Who' entry he recorded his hobby, with characteristic chutzpah, as 'organising the middle classes' and was probably the only millionaire ever to be a member of the General Council of the TUC.

Jock Stallard

An engineer and active trade unionist from Paisley near Glasgow, Albert 'Jock' Stallard was elected St Pancras councillor in 1953. Stallard was a staunch ally of John Lawrence on the council and was expelled from the Labour Party in 1958. He was readmitted to the party in the early 1960s and became a Camden councillor and then MP for St Pancras North in 1970. He was made a peer by Michael Foot. A staunch Catholic, Stallard opposed reforms to the abortion laws, gay rights and embryo research.

Dr Santo Jeger

Jeger was a Jewish GP from south Wales and politics seemed almost literally to be in the family DNA – his brother George was also a Labour MP. A rationalist, radical, passionate left-winger he had been a councillor in Shoreditch in the East End of London and member of the London County Council (LCC) since the late 1920s. Jeger was very much at the centre of the physical, turbulent politics of the 1930s. In one LCC election Jeger was opposed by a British Union of Fascists (BUF) candidate called William Joyce. As a paid official of the BUF, and with a massive scar from mouth to ear (the result of street fighting with communists), Joyce was an instantly identifiable figure. But it was his sinister, drawling voice which most people recognised. When the war broke out, Joyce fled to Germany where he became part of the Nazi propaganda machine; known mockingly in Britain as 'Lord Haw-Haw' because of his upper-class drawl, Joyce made regular radio broadcasts which were intended to undermine morale in the UK. In 1946 he was tried and hanged; he was one of the last people to be executed by the British state for treason. Jeger's anti-fascist action was not confined to combating the BUF in the East End. When the Spanish military – supported by Hitler and Mussolini – attempted to overthrow the democratically elected republican government in the summer of 1936, the ensuing civil war quickly became a cause célèbre. Like Vietnam or Iraq in more modern times, the conflict in Spain drew in a generation and defined their politics. Jeger knew where he stood from the start: he helped found the Medical Aid for Spain committee and then drove humanitarian supplies to the republican zone. Jeger's energy and enthusiasm inspired those around him. The highly influential economist and social critic R. H. Tawney praised his 'burning sincerity .... one left him with the feeling that one had been in the company of a man who not only expounded his political creed with knowledge and force but who also lived it'. Jeger continued to work in the East End as a doctor even after he became an MP. He told the voters at the 1951 general election that 'as a practising doctor ... I am kept very near the difficulties which confront people today. This has influenced me very much in my attitude in Parliament and in particular it leads me to speak out against the recent economies in the health services.' Jeger's political career was never to fully develop, however, because he died suddenly of a heart attack in September 1953.

Lena Jeger

After Santo Jeger's death, the parliamentary seat was contested at the by-election on 19 November 1953 by the late MP's widow, Lena Jeger. The daughter of a postman, Lena Jeger studied modern languages at the University of London and was a talented linguist. Her fluent Russian led to wartime service at the British embassy in Moscow and she subsequently became a journalist at the *Manchester Guardian*. In St Pancras, she was heavily involved in running the family planning service and was a leading campaigner for reform of the abortion law. She was also both a St Pancras councillor and member of the LCC. After her husband's death, Lena Jeger was the obvious choice as candidate – regional officers of the Labour Party helpfully ensured that hers was the only name to go before the General Management Committee. But this was no party stitch-up. At a time when female MPs were still a rarity, her sharp mind and evident track record of work in the local community made Jeger a popular choice. According to the memoirs of fellow female Labour MP Jean Mann, Jeger saw off 'quite a number of carpet-baggers who were after the constituency ... because those closest to the hard-working doctor knew his wife and her worth'.

Jeger won the seat at the by-election by 1,976, increasing her husband's majority by 200. Labour MP and diarist Richard Crossman recorded in his diary that the Tory government was apparently more upset about this result than Labour had initially realised, interpreting it as another sign that the country was slowly turning against them. The Holborn and St Pancras South constituency remained marginal, however, and was not a base that Jeger or Labour could take for granted. Jeger held the seat at the 1955 election, although her majority slipped to just under 1,000. In 1959 the seat was lost to the Tory television personality Geoffrey Johnson-Smith, by 656 votes. Jeger regained it again in

1964 and remained the MP for the area until she stood down in 1979 (*see* chapter 6).

Kenneth Robinson

Kenneth Robinson was the MP for St Pancras North. Robinson left school aged fifteen after his father died and was working as an insurance clerk when the Second World War broke out. He joined the Royal Navy as a rating but had what was then described as 'a good war' and by the end of hostilities he had been promoted to lieutenant-commander despite his lack of more than the basic formal education. After the war, Robinson became a St Pancras councillor and then entered parliament after a by-election for the St Pancras North seat in 1949. Robinson was particularly interested in mental health: he campaigned on decriminalising suicide in the 1950s and became the first Chair of the mental health charity Mind. He was also an active campaigner for homosexual law reform in the 1950s and an executive member of the Homosexual Law Reform Society. Robinson also campaigned strongly for reform of the abortion laws and was Minister of Health when parliament finally legalised abortion in 1967 (*see* chapter 3).

Geoffrey Johnson-Smith

Conservative counsellor in St Pancras and heart-throb television presenter in the 1950s on the BBC current affairs programme *Tonight*. When Cliff Mitchelmore put his back out, Johnson-Smith took over the anchor's chair for a few weeks in 1959 and became a household name. This exposure and the chaos in the local Labour Party helped him take the parliamentary seat in a famous victory for the Tories in the general election that year.